LADY KILLER

a novella
by
Jeff Richards

MINT HILL BOOKS
MAIN STREET RAG PUBLISHING COMPANY
CHARLOTTE, NORTH CAROLINA

Library of Congress Control Number: 2019934270

ISBN: 978-1-59948-738-0

Produced in the United States of America

Mint Hill Books
Main Street Rag Publishing Company
PO Box 690100
Charlotte, NC 28227
www.MainStreetRag.com

To Connie, Ben, and Hannah,
the Stork Club, and the Republic of Takoma Park
With love and affection

My fault, my failure, is not in the passions I have,
but in my lack of control of them.

~Jack Kerouac

The fault lies not in the stars, but in ourselves.

~William Shakespeare

Chapter One

Mitch Lovett steers his banged-up Saab up the driveway of the house he used to live in. The children pile out of the back. Addie, his four-year old, waves her hands in the air in a musical pantomime. She sings over and over again,

London Bridge is falling down,
Falling down,
Falling down...

Six-year-old Julian crosses his arms and scowls at his father as he steps out of the car. "It isn't fair that you made me come home in the middle of Grand Theft Auto. I could've beat Larry." He kicks a soccer ball in the driveway—it hits the garage door and bounces off the hood of the Saab. Mitch catches the ball as it comes down.

"You need to control your temper. Or would you like a time out?" Even as he asks the question, he feels guilty that he left the kids at the Spicer house the night before because he wanted to spend the night with Dee Wynn. What kind of father is he?

Julian must've sensed his doubt. "You don't live here. How can you give me a time out?" he grouses. He sits on the ground in protest.

"You get up, son," says his father.

"Yes, you get up. You be nice to your daddy," agrees Addie, shaking her fist at her brother. Julian defers to his younger sister. He is, like his father, a great lover of the opposite sex.

"Now, the two of you head upstairs," says Mitch with a wave of his hand. "Your mother's waiting."

He sees Kathy, the woman he once loved, crack open the front door and gaze out. She smiles gaily, and her eyes glow, but not for Mitch. The kids gallop up the stairs to hug her. "I haven't seen you forever," she says, gathering them in her arms until they start to giggle. She attended a conference in Richmond with her fellow shrinks and drove home that morning. Her antenna must be up.

"You saw us the day before yesterday," says Julian as he rushes in the house, followed by Addie.

Mitch yanks the kids' overnight bags out of the trunk and hefts them up the front steps to the hallway.

"I know something you don't know," says Kathy, looking at him carefully like he's a specimen under glass.

Mitch drops the bags in the front hallway. "What would that be?" he asks, hesitating. He eyes his ex, warily.

"Oh, come in," she says, dragging him by the arm to the living room. He sits down on the flowered sofa, which had been there since they had purchased it from the decorator at Ethan Allen before the kids were born. Kathy saunters into the kitchen to fetch two cups of coffee and a salted oatmeal cookie, which she must have purchased just for him. What is she up to? He wonders. Usually they go their separate ways until the next visitation.

Mitch looks around the room. He is amazed at how things are the same. The same two paintings hang on the wall—in the first, a woman cradles flowers in her arms as she steps out of an orange pick-up while a man behind the wheel stares at the bucolic landscape, perhaps to avoid looking at the roadside cross that dominates the foreground. In the second, a Morris Minor is poised to pull out of a country lane into the shadow of an oncoming truck. He and Kathy both love realism of the more edgy variety. They love art deco, as evidenced by the clock on the mantel that cost a fortune and the brass chandelier with the amber fleurette shades that cost nothing. (A friend was about to lower it into the trash in his condo.) The house itself was Craftsman style, with built-in wood cabinets to either side of the fireplace where Kathy kept the Waterford glasses that they received as wedding presents. He remembers purchasing all these items and how excited they were at the time, especially about the home, Kathy saying, "This is where we are going to raise our children," though they were both anxious since she'd already had two miscarriages.

Mitch is checking out a photograph of Bob and Kathy sitting in a Paris café on their honeymoon, the Champs-Élysées in the background, when Kathy slips in with her booty balanced on a silver tray. She sets the tray down on the mission-style coffee table, another item they acquired together. He sips the tea and munches the cookie, savoring every crunchy bite. He used to eat a whole package in one day, and Kathy would say, "You'll make yourself fat." But that's not true. Maybe in his fifties, but right now he's still a lady killer, bronzed skinned, muscular, and curly haired in the same mysterious Gallic way as his father and grandfather before him and so on into the misty past.

"So, what is it you know that I don't know?" he asks, grabbing another cookie.

"Dee called me this morning to tell me that you spent the night together."

He isn't sure what to say—Dee is part of his and Kathy's extended circle of friends from high school, which still gets together on a regular basis. He didn't know them until he was a freshman in college, but now he is tight with them as well, so tight that he is dating (or at least sleeping with) his ex-wife's best friend—what's more, Dee had once been engaged to Bob, Kathy's new husband. What a mess, he thinks, and shrugs.

"What does that mean? You slept with her?"

"Yes."

"Where were the kids?"

"I left them with the Spicers."

"You didn't use up all the Stork Club tickets?"

The Stork Club was their baby-sitting co-op that they started with their friends. He took the kids to a meeting of the club. Then he planned to take them to a movie and an overnight afterward, but Dee called.

"Yes, I did. I can't very well take the kids to Dee's condo."

Kathy chuckles. "Smart thinking."

"I'm glad you think so."

"Well," she says. She puts on her glasses as if to read her ex more intently. Before the kids were born she wore contacts, but they were impractical, she said. They gave her a startled look that might frighten the newborns. He found this funny but he knew better than to tell her this. It would send her off on an analytical riff.

Kathy clears her throat. "The two of you together. I think it's wonderful," she says, leaning forward and patting him lightly on the knee. "I couldn't think of a better solution. I know Julian loves Dee and she is good friends with Bob"—they were once engaged—"and Addie, she can adapt to anything."

"How about you?"

"Me," she laughs, putting down her coffee cup, a lipstick stain on the edge. "I'm a lapsed Catholic. No more guilt."

Mitch wanders out to the backyard, where his kids are playing on the swing set that he set up—when was it? A thousand years ago. He hugs the two. Addie clings to his legs. "I love you, Daddy. I love you," she says in her sorrowful voice that Mitch thinks is a little put on. She is already a drama queen.

"When will we see you again?" asks Julian, scowling at his shoes.

"I don't know, a week, I think. I'll call you."

He heads around the side of the house, avoiding Kathy, jumps in the car, and screeches out of the driveway. He is over the divorce. He is over Bob moving into the house on Woodland a month later. He is not over losing his kids, but he is trying to soften the blow through sex. It's the one thing that he can rely on. Women love him—in particular, one woman, Dee Wynn. They made love three times last night in a very lustful fashion, the third in the shower. He had her up against the tiled-wall. She was straddling his legs. Bouncing up and down. The wall was slick so they were moving from side to side as well. It was like he was in an earthquake, unsure of his footing. He noticed a bar of soap underfoot. He kicked it away and shouldered open the shower door. They toppled on top of her bed, finished the job they were working on, and fell back, satiated.

"Remember when we were in college and we double-dated with Kathy and her boyfriend, Darren McCall?" Dee asked as he stumbled out of bed to get dressed. He could see her in the mirror, smiling sleepily at him. "I was so jealous of the attention you were giving Kathy that I jumped in the front seat of Darren's car and flirted with him all the way to the dorms. And Kathy, that vixen, invited you up to her dorm room out of pure spite."

"Yep, I remember," he said, but as he recalled, it wasn't spite exactly. Kathy seemed to like him, and the next day they went out to *The Last Detail*, a flick that was perhaps too suggestive for a first date.

Dee padded over to where he stood in front of the mirror, put her arms around his chest, and squeezed tightly. She was still naked, and he could feel her breasts against his back. "Well, she had you then," said Dee, running her hand down to his stomach. "I have you now, and I'm never going to let you go."

Mitch thinks about those words now, driving home. He doesn't know whether it was a threat or a promise. He finds the lady enticing in the physical sense—Dee is a pale-skinned beauty with a lush figure—but she is no Ophelia, not a shrinking violet. She is used to getting what she wants, and he doesn't know whether he wants to be wanted, at least right now.

Mitch drives east on New Hampshire Avenue, a four-lane thoroughfare full of traffic. On either side of the road are strip malls, brand new fifty years ago, now gone to seed, a few deserted storefronts, lopsided signs, bargain stores: Mattress Discounter, Dollar Store, and Shopper's Food Warehouse. On the top of the hill on the right behind a Wendy's and Jiffy Wash is his house, which sits off by itself on a small road that borders the eastern end of Old Town.

He drives up Oak Lane to number thirteen, and parks in the gravel driveway. He stares at a dapper old man with a pencil mustache polishing the chrome on his Lincoln Town Car across the street. He has seen this man before but he's not sure where. A good looking gent. Gives him the creeps. Mitch unlocks the door, trudges up the narrow stairs to his bedroom, and collapses on his bed, one of the many wood veneer pieces he acquired from a local motel furniture outlet. He dozes off. It has been a long night.

He awakes when the alarm goes off. It's four in the afternoon. He jumps out of bed and picks out his work clothes and hangs them on a chair, but he cannot find his Rockport cordovans. He takes the room apart until he comes to the closet where, behind a small metal box that he tosses on the bed, he locates the shoes. They are four years old, worn and cracked but well-polished, his favorite for work. He may buy a new pair, but not for a while. Mitch is not comfortable with change.

He tosses the shoes on the chair, throws off his old clothes, and runs for the shower. The water comes out of the showerhead in fits and starts. The pipes bang. The house is old, the antithesis of the Craftsman-style bungalow on Woodland. It is a wafer-thin box. The exterior is painted the mellow green of a doctor's waiting room and the window trim's black. Inside the house is dark, painted an ashen gray like there might have been smoke damage at some point. The radiators rattle, and the floors creak. Julian and Addie told their mother the house was haunted. They didn't want to sleep there another night. Kathy agreed they didn't have to and made it clear to Mitch that the kids had enough trauma with the divorce—why add to it?

"Where am I going to take them for overnights?"

"You can take them to the Crowne Plaza. They love it there," she said, and he had to finally agree because the last thing he wanted was to rock the boat any more than it is rocking right now.

The Crowne Plaza in Rockville, a known hangout for recently divorced dads, was the first place he moved after he was kicked out of the house. He did this at the advice of a colleague who'd gone through the same experience, and, like the colleague, he stayed for a short time until he could find a place near his kids. He knew he shouldn't have purchased this house—it is a dump—but number thirteen Oak Lane was zoned commercial. A developer owned the parcels on either side of him, and the scuttlebutt was that the developer planned to sell the land to a hardware chain. He figures that he will make a killing.

Mitch is good at investments, though he is not good at keeping a steady job. Not that he's a screw-up—he just can't stand still. He quit the job at CNN because it kept him behind the camera in the studio. He saved up enough money to start his own business. After that he was always gone, filming in Europe and the Middle East and as far away as Siberia, where he shot a piece about the Siberian wolf for *National Geographic.* That's what caused the divorce. Kathy's private practice suffered during that time; she said she felt like a single mother. She wanted a spouse to help out, not a globetrotter. That's where Bob Johnson fit in. He designs projects for the Air and Space Museum and writes books about rocket science. He is a mental giant, like Kathy's father, and like him as well, he keeps regular hours.

Mitch jumps out of the shower and dries himself. The ironic thing was that after they separated and he moved to the Crowne Plaza, he stopped traveling. He was suffering from a deep funk. He begged Kathy to relent on her decision—it was her idea, after all, this separation, but she refused. She said with finality, "You've made your bed, and now you'll have to lie in it." He shakes his head and laughs at himself in the mirror. Mitch's father was married four times. His mother was number two. She died. He left town in search of another mate. Mitch's fondest wish has always been not to follow in the old man's footsteps. Now it seems that he will.

He brushes his teeth, shrugs as if to say, "I'll deal with this later." He makes a muscle in the mirror.

Mitch slips into a new pair of chinos, a blue-and-white-striped polo, his comfortable Rockports. As he picks up his camera, he hears a knock on the door. Heads down the narrow stairs to the hallway. Looks through the peephole. It's Gail Strickland, a friend that he has known since college.

He opens the door.

"Hi," she says, tentatively, looking behind him in the house as though checking for company. "I hope I'm not disturbing you."

"No, come in," he says. "I do have to leave in half an hour. I have a very precise shoot in Georgetown. I have to film the sun going down."

"Oh, that sounds interesting."

"It's an ad for a seafood restaurant. It puts money in my pocket."

He shows her to a plastic sofa in the living room that Mitch covered with a soft blanket because he hated the way his skin peeled off the material. She wears a low-cut Danskin that clings tightly to the contours of her body. He can see the outline of her bra. As he watches, sweat slides down between her breasts. What is going on with him? All of a sudden, he seems like a beast on the prowl.

Gail is a friend that he has known since college, introduced, of course, by Dee Wynn but this was after he met his former wife. He has always felt strongly attracted to her in the same way he feels attracted to Kathy. A way he can't explain, as much mental as physical. Not the way he feels about Dee.

"Ed and Davy are watching an Orioles game at Bull's house," she says. "I have to pick them up in an hour anyway."

Ed is her husband, a former jock and the present assistant coach at Montgomery Blair High School. He is known for his hair-trigger temper.

"How are you doing?" Gail asks, putting a hand on Mitch's knee lightly.

"I'm fine. A fair amount of work," he responds, putting his hand on top of hers.

"Dee called me this morning. She said you spent the night with her."

Mitch withdraws his hand, laughs. "That woman's crazy. She called Kathy too."

"She's not crazy," says Gail. "She's like a cat. Marking her territory."

"Yep, well, you and Kathy are inaccessible. No need to warn you."

"I know we don't need to be warned, but maybe you do. Dee's a good person, but she can be controlling." Gail smiles demurely, eyes downcast like the coy mistress of Marvell's poem.

They sit there for a long moment, a heavy weight in the air. The Gail he knew in college was more focused. A history major. Worked for an antique dealer in Georgetown after she graduated. She seemed happier then, and he knows why, though it makes him feel uneasy. He changes the subject.

"How are you doing?"

"Ed and I got in a terrific fight over a hunting trip he's taking with his buddies to Western Maryland. I wanted to join them. We'd leave David with Robin and Barry. He insisted that we shouldn't use up all the Stork Club tickets at once," Gail says, a glint of disdain in her eyes, "besides none of the other women are invited on the hunting trip."

She shakes her head. "So I told him that I could invite the women, but he dug in his heels. I didn't understand, he said, it's a sacred thing, and the other women won't agree. They know that they need to give their husbands space. I said, I understand as well, but you never take me anywhere. And this made him so mad that he kicked a hole in the wall."

"Maybe you should send him to anger management classes."

"Yeah right. When hell freezes over. But I did get him to agree to take me on a camping trip some other weekend. I'd rather go to a bed and breakfast somewhere but, you know, beggars can't be choosers."

Gail takes her hand off his knee and reaches in her purse. "Oh, yes, I have something to show you. I know how much you love history. I found this at a street fair on Capitol Hill."

She hands him a Confederate five-dollar bill wrapped in plastic, points at a gaunt goateed gent in the illustration.

"Jefferson Davis," she says, pointing also at a crease in the bill. "My guess is that it was once folded in a wallet."

She tells Mitch that they found a five-dollar Davis bill in Lincoln's wallet after he died. "Could be the same one."

"Yeah, sure. You know the chances of that." They both laugh. He returns the bill. Their hands touch. They look into each other's eyes. But then Mitch remembers his appointment, looks down at his watch. "Got to go," he says.

"Yes," says Gail with what he imagines as relief. "Me too."

Mitch totes his camera outside. Puts it in the backseat. Covers it with a blanket. Expensive equipment. He doesn't want it stolen. He wanders over to Gail Strickland who's standing by her husband's black Nissan pickup, keys in hand. He hugs her.

"Hey, I enjoyed seeing you today. I mean seriously, if you need to talk again, I'm here," he says, thinking at the same time, *what am I, nuts?*

Chapter Two

ail Strickland takes a left on New Hampshire Avenue. She feels stupid. Why did she barge in on Mitch? Is she seeking solace because her relationship with Ed stinks? Why not barge in on Kathy? Or Robin? Why not someone of her own sex who understands where she is coming from? The answer is simple: she is attracted to the man. His soft hazel eyes; his carefree smile; his thick, tousled, dark chocolate hair; his angular jaw; his dimpled chin; his bronzed complexion; and his tight, compact body, broad shouldered and muscular. He might as well be D'Artagnan of the Three Musketeers. All he lacks is a turned-up mustache and a feathered, tricorn hat. And there is something else as well, a connection they seemed to share since the first time Dee introduced him and he looked into her eyes with such intensity, she could feel her heart race. Her thoughts turn to yesterday at the Stork Club meeting— Mitch looked at her from across the room with the same dark intensity.

Then Dee called this morning to say she slept with Mitch— the bastard, to sleep with that bitch. Makes Gail feel violated, that the intensity she saw in his eyes was biological, that of a dog in heat, not something deeper. He is no different than every other joker she's ever known, and that puts her in mind of the worst joker of all, the one at the University of Denver who got her pregnant in her sophomore year and promised to marry her. He rushed her to the hospital two months early. She was bleeding profusely. They wheeled her into the operating room, and when she awoke hours later, all stitched up, the joker was gone and the baby dead.

She takes a left on Ethan Allan, follows 410 to Birch. Parks the car in front of Bull's house, a dinky rental with a tiny yard, wedged between two large colonials.

She sits in the Nissan. Hands on the steering wheel. Sometimes at night she can't sleep because she wonders what would have happened if the baby girl lived. Would she have the heart-shaped lips and thick, curly eyelashes of the mother, the green eyes of her father? Would Gail have married her father? This is where her imagination fails her. She hates the father of the baby. She wonders if all men are the same—jokers. Say one thing, do another. Even Mitch Lovett. She slams her fist against the steering wheel.

She jumps out of the Nissan and finds David stomping up and down in a mud puddle in the backyard. His Power Ranger shoes are caked in mud, as is the seat of his new jeans. He's covered with brown specks, as though the freckles on his cheeks have reproduced themselves endlessly.

He runs up to his mother and puts his arms around her, leaving two runny brown spots on her pants.

"Mommy, I missed you. Where you been?"

"Visiting a friend."

"A boy or girl?"

"A girl," she lies. Little pitchers have big ears. Besides, she doesn't trust Ed.

It's funny how things work out. She's hot for Mitch. But before Bob moved in, she was good friends with his ex, Kathy. She sees Kathy as a model, someone with children and enough courage to leave her husband.

Gail takes Davy over to an outdoor spigot and cleans his hands. Then she takes his shoes and washes them off. She notices he's wheezing. "You feel okay? You're not short of breath?"

"No, Mommy, I'm bored," he says. "Let's do something. Let's go to Chucky Cheese."

"Davy, darling, where'd your daddy put your asthma kit?" He shrugs.

She grabs his hand and takes him inside to the TV room. Bull bends forward on the sofa, his mouth open, glassy eyed. Ed sits next to him, a shotgun in his lap, his feet propped up on a coffee table, a big grin on his face.

They're both watching an Orioles game while Barry Spicer brags about what a good car salesman he is. (He was once the manager of the Blair football team when Ed was the quarterback and likes to impress his buddies.) He is telling them about selling a fleet of Saabs to a dot-com company when Gail interrupts.

"Is that thing loaded?" she asks hesitantly.

"Of course it isn't," scoffs Bull. He was once Ed's blocking back, a big bruiser with long, stringy black hair and Fu Manchu mustache. "That there is a gift to Ed. A pump-action Winchester 12 I inherited from my dad. Show her it isn't loaded."

Ed picks up the gun and points it at the TV, where the Orioles are behind ten to one to the Royals. He pulls the trigger. It clicks. He pumps the gun. *Shack-a-lack. Shack-a-lack,* the well-oiled purr of metal sliding against metal. Another click. Gail winces.

"Would you stop that?" she asks, holding tightly to Davy, who seems fascinated by the weapon.

"What, you don't want me to blow away Bull's TV? Put the Orioles out of their misery."

They all three roll back and forth on the sofa, giggling like kids.

"You been smoking dope?" asks Gail. Bull works construction, but it's rumored he also deals marijuana. None of the heavier stuff, though that doesn't appease Gail. With the dope and the guns, she's convinced he's a bad influence. "Haven't you?"

"Hey, I can relax, can't I?" Ed says.

"Do you realize Davy was out back playing in the mud? Look how dirty he is."

He glances at his son. "There's nothing wrong with a little mud on a warm day like this." He runs his hand through the boy's hair. Davy squirms.

"Where's the asthma kit?" asks Gail.

"In the glove compartment of Bull's car." Bull tosses her his keys.

When she returns to the TV room, Bull's telling Ed and Barry about a Dragnet rerun he saw the other night where a young married couple were smoking dope and forgot that they left the water running in the bathtub and their kid, who's in the tub, drowns. "Sergeant Friday was giving them a hard time."

"Gee, I wonder why," says Gail. She makes Davy breathe in the inhalant tube.

"I'm fine, Mom," he says. "I can breathe."

"Then we better go."

"Hey, we're having fun here," says Ed, leaning forward and stretching. He thrusts the gun at her. "I mean we're celebrating the fact that Bull gave me this beautiful piece." He runs his hand across the stock. "Look at the hand-carved walnut finish, all the swirls and curlicues and the scrollwork in the metal, two ducks and a hunting dog in gold leaf. It must have cost a fortune. You ought to thank our benefactor."

"Thanks, Bull," Gail sighs, one hand on her hip as she stares sternly at her husband.

"No problem," says Bull. "I own another Model 12 that's even better. My pop purchased them from a fellow at a gun show who didn't know what he had."

"Yeah, it's a great piece," says Ed, grinning defiantly at his wife. "Nothing like the piece of junk you gave me for my last birthday."

What he is referring to is a dueling pistol she found at an antique store. He tried to make the pistol operational but couldn't; it was meant as a showpiece. He hung it on the wall for a week then angrily tossed it in the trash. She retrieved the pistol and took it to the basement to a trunk where she kept some of her antiques, the ones Ed wouldn't allow her to display in the house.

"It's getting late. You have to work tomorrow, darling," she says, trying to appear reasonable though she'd rather strangle him. "Besides, maybe Davy needs the nebulizer."

"Mom," whines the boy.

"Hey, I understand," says Bull, giving Ed a knowing look. "In a couple of weeks we'll be out hunting. Everything will be fine."

"You bet it will," says Ed as he grins at his buddies, pushes up off the couch slowly like a spring uncoiling. He hitches up his pants and strolls out to the car, reminding Gail of the old Ed Strickland. Back in the misty past, in high school, Ed gave her his surfer's cross. She was flattered that he paid attention to her. Though she didn't care for jocks, she thought he was different. The casual way he leaned out the window of his black Impala. Tilted his aviator sunglasses so she could see his gray, hawkish eyes as she drifted by. "Hey, sweetie," he said one day. "You want to go for a ride?" She hopped in the car. He screeched off. It was thrilling. They ended the night in the back seat of the car in one of the parking lots off Sligo Creek Parkway, groping each other.

But, there was a disturbing edge to his personality. He'd get in fights outside of clubs, on the football field, and near the creek behind the school where the kids smoked cigarettes. Once a kid stole a dime bag of his marijuana. He broke the kid's arm. Another time he pushed a kid down the front steps at Blair for, as he claimed, making the moves on Gail. They were only talking about homework.

Then there were the fights with his father, mostly verbal, but sometimes physical. The one she remembers best was one winter night after a snowstorm when they caught his parents arguing. Ed's dad was drunk, backing his mom up to the hot screen of the fireplace where a fire was roaring. Ed yanked his father from behind and turned him around. Mr. Strickland threw a punch at his son that caught him in the jaw. Snapped his head. Ed grabbed his father by the lapels of his jacket and threw him to the floor. Jumped on top of him. Raised his fist. But before he could deliver a blow, Mrs. Strickland grabbed his arm.

"It's not his fault," she said. Gail thought she meant because he's drunk, it's not his fault though it was something entirely different that Gail was not to find out until years later after Mr. Strickland died Nancy Strickland confessed that it wasn't his fault because she had an affair.

Gail Strickland climbs in the black Nissan. Ed's no longer grinning. He has a scowl on his face like he's another person. He yells at her all the way home about how he didn't like the way she treated him. Like he was an out-of-control dope fiend, unable to take care of his own child. He wasn't that stoned. He knew exactly what was going on. Davy was getting bored with the baseball game and asked to go outside. So he let him. He could see him from the window. He could see that he was getting dirty. Boys are allowed to get dirty.

"I know," says Gail, gripping the steering wheel tightly, staring straight ahead at the road. "I know, but still you shouldn't be smoking in front of our son."

"I wasn't," he yells. "I did it while he was taking a nap. We went in the backyard. Took a couple of tokes. So what?"

"I'm sorry. I didn't know."

"If you didn't know, you should've kept your big trap shut."

"Don't talk to me that way."

"I'll talk to you any way I fucking want to." Ed turns around in his seat, points a finger at her. "You know what the worse thing is, what pisses me off?"

"What?"

"What pisses me off is that right now, Barry and Bull are talking about what a wimp I am. To let my wife chew me out and make me go home. They think I'm pussy whipped."

"That's a disgusting expression."

"Jesus." Ed slams his fist against the dashboard. Crosses his arms. Stares out the window. "And another thing—you don't have to lecture me about guns."

"I wasn't lecturing."

"You were asking me if that gun was loaded. You think I'm enough of an idiot to carry a loaded gun around the house?"

When she parks the pickup, Ed Strickland clambers out, leans in to pick up the Model 12 he propped against the seat, and slams the door behind him. He takes the weapon to the shed, to the safe, then locks the shed door, fixes Gail with a withering glare, and then marches down the front walk, opens the front door of the house, and slams it behind him. Gail helps Davy out of his safety seat. "What's wrong with Daddy?" he asks.

Gail isn't exactly sure. What she does know is that when she returned from Colorado, six weeks after her baby died, she was a whipped dog to the point that she decided to pursue Ed Strickland until he agreed to marry her. It must've been temporary insanity considering what's happened since. It wasn't love. It may've been desire. But whatever it was, she finished her degree at Maryland. Ed's football career fizzled out, and, when he graduated without prospects, they married and Ed's father arranged the Blair job.

Five years later Ed's father died. His mother sold the house and moved to her family home in North Carolina, where she told Gail one night after the boys were tucked in bed that she shouldn't have told her husband about the affair but she was consumed with guilt at the time. Her sister had an affair at about the same time and didn't breathe a word to Chuck—as far as she knew they were as happy as clams. You have to be careful with men, she said, patting Gail's knee gently. They have fragile egos.

Gail fixes dinner, vegetarian chili and salad for her and Ed, a can of Dinosaurs and mixed fruit for Davy. He eats only processed food. She serves the meal in the dining room. Ed watches 60 Minutes as he shovels the chili down before attacking the salad.

Gail sits at the table, her fork poised above the salad. She doesn't want to antagonize Ed, but maybe there's a way, after his hunting trip with Bull, she could convince him to go to a bed and breakfast rather than camping like he wants.

"No way," he says after she introduces the subject.

"It's much more romantic," she says, putting the fork down and squeezing his arm, "we can get to know each other all over again."

"We can get to know each other in the woods," says Ed, eyes still intent on the TV.

"The ground is too hard. I like a nice, warm bed."

"We can't afford it." He switches the TV channel to the local news.

"What does that mean? Two nights at a bed and breakfast can't be that expensive."

"You want to go to one of those places, you pay for it. Get a fucking job." He glares at her.

She glares back, pissed. She had a job before he suggested she quit to take care of Davy. She is about to remind him of her sacrifice, but he has turned his full attention back to the TV.

"Why don't you turn that thing off?" she snaps, but then she doesn't give him a chance. She turns it off for him.

"What'd you do that for?"

Davy pushes his plate off the table. Canned fruit and dinosaurs splatter on the carpet. "I hate this food," he cries. "I want to go to Chucky Cheese."

Gail looks down at the spilled plate. Her eyes follow a red line of tomato paste across the carpet to Ed's new tennis shoes. In the middle of the left shoe is a big red splotch. Ed too looks down at his shoe. He places his fork down carefully and then reaches over with his open hand to smack Davy in the head, but Gail grabs him by the wrist before he can deliver the blow.

"Don't you dare," she says. This is not the first time he tried to smack their son, and Gail wasn't going to tolerate it.

Davy is still screaming about how he wants to go to Chucky Cheese. "I want the pizza. I want pepperoni and sausage on the pizza."

Gail holds her husband by the wrist. They glare at each other. Then he yanks his wrist away, pushes himself up from the table, and storms out of the house, slamming the door behind him.

Davy stops screaming long enough to ask what's wrong with Daddy. Gail scoops the dinosaurs and fruit back on the plate. She wipes up the tomato paste.

"Your daddy is mad at you because you spilled your food on the floor."

"I want to go to Chucky Cheese."

"You can't go to Chucky Cheese," she says. She takes the plate into the kitchen, comes back with paper towels and Resolve. Dabs all the red stains on the carpet.

"I want pepperoni-and-sausage pizza."

She takes Davy by the hand and leads him into his room.

"Are we going to Chucky Cheese?" he asks.

"No, you're going in here for a four-minute time-out. You shouldn't throw your food on the floor."

Davy starts blubbering, but he obeys his mother and stays in his room. She closes the door behind him. She heads for the kitchen where she cleans the dishes. Ed punches open the back door and saunters in, a big grin on his face. She can smell smoke in his clothes.

"You've been smoking dope," she says.

"Get off my back." He still grins, paws in his pockets.

She decides not to pursue it, asks instead if she can clean the tomato paste off his tennis shoe.

"I've already done it. In the spigot out back," he says, putting one of his paws on her shoulder and squeezing. "You know, I was thinking. Maybe we can put Davy to bed early and head in the bedroom to have some fun."

"I don't think so. I'm tired," she says, turning away from him to the kitchen sink where she starts loading the dishwasher. "Besides, I can't understand why you want to after our fighting."

"We'll make up."

He creeps up behind her. Grabs her around the waist and leans down to kiss her on the neck. She makes a slight squirming motion as if to loosen his grip and, though it is involuntary—it is his breathing on her neck that causes her to squirm, it raises Ed's ire.

"I'm just a guy wants to fuck his wife. Anything wrong with that?" he growls as he shoves her against the edge of the kitchen counter and strides out of the room.

Chapter Three

Mitch Lovett leans against the windowsill in his bedroom looking out at the Jiffy Wash across the street where the same dapper old man with a pencil mustache that he saw a couple of days ago polishes the chrome on his Lincoln Town car. Or maybe it's not the same man. But whoever it is, it gives him the creeps and makes him think of his father who once sported a pencil mustache, a homburg tilted rakishly on his head, and an initialed briefcase—always off to somewhere else, that's the image Mitch carries of his old man. He doesn't know where this old dapper man is headed but he knew where his dad was headed, to the comfort of some lady's bed. That's the last thing Mitch wants for himself. Yet here he is, recently divorced, waiting for a married lady to show up at his doorstep. It's his own fault. He invited her to call him, and she did. He sees the black Nissan pickup inching its way up Oak Lane, and he hustles down the stairs to the front door.

Gail Strickland parks under the overhanging branches of the willow tree on his street and wanders up the cracked sidewalk to the house. Mitch opens the door.

"What? Oh!" He blinks. "Sunlight."

"I'm not too early, am I?" asks Gail in a soft voice he can barely make out.

"No, no." He takes her by the arm and leads her in. Sticks his head out, checks up and down the street, and catches the eye of the dapper old man. The old man winks at Mitch. Mitch slams the door behind him.

Gail stands in the dark hallway, arms folded across her chest, shivering.

"Have you eaten breakfast?"

"No."

They head into the kitchen. Gail sits down at the table; its top is plastic made to look like knotty pine. The chair tilts slightly. The floor is uneven, covered in linoleum that is cracked and peeling off, exposing the wood floorboards underneath.

"I hope you'll pardon this old funky mess. It's temporary," says Mitch, opening the kitchen window. A hot wind blows in from the woods. The birds twitter in the trees behind the house, and the traffic on New Hampshire hums in the distance. He opens the refrigerator and eyes a six-pack of beer, a carton of eggs, and two blocks of cheese—one moldy—green peppers, onions, margarine, and orange marmalade. He snickers. "I'm not always a slob."

"I know you're not," says Gail, squirming in her seat. She stands up, peers down at the chair, pulls up a tack, and shows it to him.

"I think I was sitting on this," she says, laughing. She seems to relax.

"Oh, I'm sorry," says Mitch. "The Ritz this ain't."

Mitch fumbles around the kitchen while Gail shows him her latest finds: a small Civil War tin cup—part of a mess kit—and a blue ceramic vase with the initials VL at the bottom. "If this turns out to be a Victoria Littlejohn, I'll sell it. Could get as much as seven hundred dollars."

"That's impressive," says Mitch as he pulls down a bowl from a shelf, breaks some eggs for an omelet. "What are you going to do with the tin cup?"

"Oh, I don't know. Maybe put it on the mantelpiece. Put some flowers in it."

He laughs, cuts up a tomato and green pepper to put in the omelet. Gail watches as he heats up a pan on the stove, tosses in the vegetables, and covers it.

"I don't mean to change the subject, but how are you and Dee doing?"

"We're not doing anything. I haven't seen her." He lifts the pan and stirs the vegetables.

"That's good. I don't think she's your type."

"Who do you think is my type?" He pours the eggs over the vegies, sprinkles Bac'n Pieces and Parmesan on top.

"I don't know, but it's probably someone more straightforward and relaxed, like your former wife."

"She was my type, but not anymore." Mitch finishes the omelet. Puts a plate down in front of Gail. Pours the coffee. Sits down across from her.

"Do you still love Kathy?" she asks as she picks at her food.

"In a way, but the truth is, I don't want to think about it. Kathy's advice is that I focus on the future. I agree."

"How do you feel about Bob Johnson?"

"Jeez, Gail," he says as he finishes his coffee and pours a half cup more. "Bob is a fine fellow, but I didn't think so at first."

"I don't mean to pry, but were they having an affair before you separated?"

"No, could you imagine Bob having an affair? He's such a wimp, he wouldn't know where to start. Why do you ask?"

"I don't know." She shrugs. She stares at her omelet, takes a couple of bites, sips her coffee, then looks up at Mitch. "That must've hurt when Bob moved in with Kathy."

"You're damn right it hurt," says Mitch. "But it taught me a lesson."

"What's that?"

"Tomorrow is another day."

"I heard that line somewhere before."

"Yeah, right." Now he's the squirmy one. He doesn't like to reveal too much about himself without reciprocation. "How about you?" he asks. "What's your story?"

"You know my story. I have a great child and a wonderful husband." She raises her eyebrows in a pensive way. "No, to be honest, they're both a pain in the ass."

"What do you mean by that?"

"I guess what I mean," says Gail, leaning forward in the chair. "If I got rid of one of them, the other would be less of a pain in the ass."

"You mean, get rid of Ed?"

"Yes, exactly."

Mitch decides that he should not pursue this line of questioning any further. He knows where it may be leading, and he's not sure that he wants to go there. At least not yet.

He finishes his omelet but finds he's still hungry. Digs in the freezer. Finds a loaf of bread behind the frozen meals. He defrosts two slices in the microwave. Toasts them. Spreads margarine and marmalade on top. Nibbles the crust. Then plunges into the heart of the bread.

"I got home late last night. I didn't eat," he says by way of explanation.

"How about you and Dee?" says Gail, leaning on her elbow and smiling tightly, as though she's upset. "I'm curious about your motives. I mean, why did you really hook up with her?"

"Oh, right," he says, trying to come up with something. "I don't know about other men, but I suspect they're like me. Your wife divorces you. You feel inadequate. Along comes a beautiful woman, in this case Dee. You make love. You feel better. You're not a total loser."

"Boy, you make it sound so easy. Using a woman to make you feel better," says Gail, shaking her head as though she's impressed.

"I'm being honest. That's all," says Mitch. "I like Dee. She's a good friend, and I don't see anything wrong with making love to her. I'm sure you've made love to someone you don't love."

"You can bet on that," says Gail, not intending to come on so strong. She blushes.

Mitch looks at her carefully but doesn't say anything.

"I guess we better change the subject," she adds, finally.

They sit there for a long moment staring at each other, each waiting for the other to speak first. Finally, Mitch stands up. Clears the dishes off the table, even though Gail has hardly touched a thing. "You want some more coffee?"

"Yes."

He pours it for her. She takes a slow sip. Puts the cup down. "Maybe I should go."

"Why?"

"Because, I don't know, things are getting too personal. Maybe."

"You sound so definite."

"I know," she says. "This is stupid. I don't know why I came over here. I don't get along with Ed. But that doesn't mean that I should be, well, in a house alone with another man."

"Yet you're here. You want me to tell you why?" he asks rhetorically. "I know I sound like an egotist, but, I think, you're here because you're attracted to me."

"Now I know I have to go." She stares into his eyes. Doesn't stand up.

"I'm attracted to you, too." He sits down next to Gail. Their shoulders touch. "Ever since we met. Where was it?—at that keg party at Maryland. Years ago. Remember how Dee introduced us. I felt this strong attraction even though I was with Kathy."

Gail looks down at her hands. "Yeah, I know. I felt it too. But maybe you're giving me a line. Maybe it's the same line that you used on Dee. How do I know?"

"You don't know," he says, "all I can say is that I am attracted to you in an immensely strong way."

"Maybe I should go," she whispers.

"Maybe you should," he whispers back.

Mitch and Gail stand up. She tries to get around him, but he stops her. Brushes the hair out of her face. Draws her to him. He kisses her. She pushes against his chest.

"This is probably not a good idea," she murmurs.

"It's a horrible idea, considering the circumstances," he agrees kissing her with such force that she backs up against the table and knocks over the coffee cup. Coffee spills on her jeans. The cup breaks on the floor. But they don't clean up the mess.

They hurry upstairs to the bedroom instead, where they squirm out of their clothes and jump in bed. She hits her head against something hard. "Ouch," she yelps, a grimace of pain on her lips. She reaches under the covers, pulls out a metal box, and opens it before he can stop her. Inside she finds a gun and a pack of .38 caliber bullets.

She snickers nervously. "Another gun nut."

"I'm not a gun nut," he exclaims, taking the box away from her and putting it back on the shelf. "I have the gun because, well…"

"Protection."

"Not exactly." He shrugs. "I purchased it on a whim because…well, I wanted to murder Bob Johnson. But then I decided that was a stupid idea. I didn't want to spend the rest of my life in jail or ruin my kid's lives. Divorce is bad enough."

"Then why don't you throw the gun away?" she asks, rubbing her head.

"I will one day. Not this very second." He leans down and kisses the spot where her head hit the metal box. He runs his lips down her neck to her shoulder to her breasts.

"I didn't mean…oh-h-h," she moans, pressing his face to her breasts gently and begging him to kiss harder. He does. His tongue tickles her nipple. She moans. Arches her back like a cat settling down in a pool of sunlight. He reaches between her legs and pushes his finger inside her. He tickles her until she's wet. She moans again, this time with more abandon. She whispers in his ear, "yes, yes, yes," words he loves to hear. He clambers on top of her too eagerly and thrusts his pecker inside too quickly, as it turns out, because she is as slippery as one of those slippery slides that kids water down on hot days, and he skids all the way down the slide without any control. She grabs his ass as he pulls back to make another plunge, and she pushes him down that slide so fast that when he hits bottom, she jumps less from passion than surprise as he lets loose with the torrent.

"You came," she gasps in a crestfallen voice. "Oh, jeez."

"Yes, too quickly," he says, lying down on his back beside her. "But I have so much desire for you that it's hard for me to control."

"Oh, that's nice," she says turning on her side and running her hand through his hair and telling him the same time that he ought to keep his mind off sex. Think of baseball, football, or elephants in the zoo. It doesn't matter. Men have a tendency to ejaculate too soon because they are too focused in on their own pleasure and not enough on their partners. She reminds him of a teacher in a soft-porn film, propping herself up on one elbow to instruct him.

He laughs. "I know all these things," he says. "I'm forty-three, coming out of a fourteen-year marriage. You don't think I learned something along the way?"

"I'm sorry. I didn't mean to insult you," she says, tears coming to her eyes unexpectedly like she is the one who's hurt.

"Don't worry," he says. "I meant it when I said I have so much feeling for you, so much desire, that it's hard for me to hold back."

"You did?" She seems surprised.

"Don't underestimate yourself," he says, squeezing her shoulder gently. "You're a smart woman, a beautiful woman. Everything a man could desire."

She leans over and kisses him, and then their kissing becomes more passionate and he's inside her, sliding up and down that slippery slide but with more control, his mind on baseball, his mouth on hers, little pecks followed by big sloppy kisses and back to pecks until he drifts back to what is actually transpiring.

"It's about three in the afternoon. I have to leave soon," she says as she settles down on top of his crotch like a cat making room on a pillow. She bounces up and down smoothly. Her breasts are small. Rosy red nipples like he's seen in a picture of Marilyn Monroe. Only he read somewhere that hers were painted on. Gail's, he assumes, are real. He reaches up and squeezes her breasts, tweaks her nipples between his fingers. She moans. Bounces up and down in a more rapid motion. He tenses the muscles of his legs, pushes up as she comes down. They seem to have a rhythm going, but he doesn't feel close enough to her, so he rises up and flips her onto the bed gently so he's on top of her. She wraps her legs around his back. She is purring like a kitten. Then, as the rhythm increases, their flesh slaps together, their lips mingle in wet kisses, and a guttural purr rises from her throat. Her whole body tenses. He pushes in as hard as he can, then out and in again until she is practically wailing. She begs him to come and when he does, their bodies shiver like two motors grinding to a halt.

"I guess I underrated you," she says as they slip on their clothes.

"Hey, ditto," says Mitch, "seems like we're very compatible."

They wander down the stairs quietly, as if to savor the cozy feeling that has descended upon them.

"We're compatible," she says as she reaches the front door and turns around to face him. "But we need to level with each other. I'm not like Dee to you, am I?"

"No, it's more than a physical attraction, I think," says Mitch, scratching his head thoughtfully. "I'm not in any way attuned to Dee like I am to you. I mean, I think we have a connection that's deeper. We both love history, for instance."

She laughs. "That's true. That's true. But what else makes you think that our connection is deeper?"

"I don't know. We both love our kids? Is that enough?"

"I suppose though a…"—she moves closer to him—"for right now, you can just say 'I had a delightful experience, and I think you are a delightful person.'"

"I had a delightful experience, and I think you are a delightful person," says Mitch, smiling. "And, I might add, delectable."

She leans up and pecks him on the cheek. "I think you're delectable as well," she says. She opens the front door and hurries out to the black Nissan. Across the street at the car wash, two men in galoshes look up from shining the bumper of a Mustang and stare at Gail. One of them whistles and winks at Mitch. He mouths some words that Mitch can't make out, but he imagines it's something like, "You, lucky dog."

Gail glances at the men. They grin back at her. She ducks behind the wheel and drives off.

Chapter Four

Dee Wynn checks her legs in the full-length mirror in the bathroom of her condo on New Hampshire Avenue. She thinks they are too muscular, almost masculine; though all the men she has been with say that she has beautiful legs. She doesn't believe them. She leans close to the mirror to put on make-up. She rides the elevator down to the lobby and walks through the glass doors to the sidewalk. As she dodges the pedestrians and traffic, a plume of smoke from a bus attacks her nostrils. A beamer honks at her as she crosses the street. Heat waves rise from the pavement even though the sun is low in the sky. She can see a streak of red on the horizon above the buildings.

Dee is thirty-nine, a principal at her architecture firm. She loves her job, which involves renovating public buildings, such as Union Station, to their former glory. She took part in the design of Washington Harbor, a series of postmodern structures facing the Potomac River, a mix of Gothic Revival, Victorian, art deco, and Neoclassical designs. It pulls together all the different elements of architecture in Georgetown. An amazing piece of work, she thinks, far superior to the Kennedy Center or the Watergate complex. Now she is working on a monument to disabled veterans that will end up on the National Mall if it passes Congress.

Dee heads down the escalator to the cool darkness of the Metro. She takes the train toward Takoma Park, where she's to meet her friends for a girls' night out. Most of her friends are married with kids, but this did not upset Dee until lately. Her biological clock is running down. From the time she was a youngster, she thinks, looking out the window as the lights flash by in the dark tunnel, she was single-minded in pursuit of her vocation. This came from her parents. Her dad was a medical researcher at NIH, her Mom a gynecologist. They arrived home late at night. They preached the work ethic to her. They also gave her responsibility early, the care of Dee's six younger siblings with the part-time help of a nanny. She changed diapers. She fixed dinner. She knew what it was like to be a mother before most of her Stork Club friends knew what it was like to kiss a boy.

It's this childcare that soured her toward children. She considers it messy and distracting. Dee wants more than anything else in the world to live a reasonable life. Perhaps she is selfish. But she can see no logic in raising six children, as did her parents, or three, for that matter. Her brother, the dentist, told her, "never let them outnumber you." But she would go even further than that. One is the perfect number. That way you could pass the child back and forth, leaving a more reasonable amount of time for your own wants. She would want the father to be Mitch Lovett, of course. What a perfect little family, even with Mitch's other kids visiting on occasion. She likes Julian, who is a serious little boy, and Mia—though she is highly strung, she is sweet and kind. Perhaps Dee has come to the point in her life where she wants to be a part of a family again. She looks out the window and sees a reflection of herself smiling dreamily.

When she arrives at Republic—on top of the hill on Laurel Street—Kathy, Robin, Gail, and Sonya are sitting in the red velvet booth in the bay window at the front of the bistro-style restaurant. They are leaning close in to each other gabbing and stirring their swizzle sticks in their drinks like Macbeth's witches when they see Dee standing beside them with a sardonic grin on her face.

"We were just talking about you," says Robin. Dee slides into the booth next to Kathy.

Republic is a new restaurant, so named to reflect the lefty character of the town. Long stainless steel bar, roughhewn wood tables and metal chairs, industrial lighting, gold beaux-arts wallpaper taken from a genuine Paris bistro. The People's

Republic of Takoma Park, as it is sometimes called in jest, was backwoods hippie when Dee was growing up. Now it is upscale, lefty chic.

Sonya giggles. "We were saying that isn't it amazing that you're dating Kathy's former husband and she's living with your former fiancée."

Dee turns to Kathy. "You told them about Mitch and me?"

"Well, it's not exactly a secret," says Kathy, blushing.

"What she means," says Robin, "is that Barry was at a poker game last night with some of the guys and Bull told him that he was at the Wendy's in front of Mitch's house with his girlfriend, Paula Wells, and they saw you outside in Mitch's yard. You were kissing him." She pokes Dee in the side.

"It was you, wasn't it?" asks Kathy.

"Yes, of course it was me."

Dee is lying. Never in her life has she been on Oak Lane. But she isn't about to let anyone know that some woman got the best of her with Mitch Lovett, the bastard. She feels like the foundation has been kicked out from under her. Usually it's her does the kicking, the way she did with Bob Johnson.

They order dinner, and while they are talking about family issues, Dee Wynn wonders what she has done to deserve this treatment. She has known these friends since their confirmation at Little Flower Catholic Church. They are inseparable, though Dee is the only one who hasn't fallen into line, and for a good reason. Robin Spicer married her high school sweetheart. After three children, Barry got a vasectomy, to Robin's chagrin, saying they couldn't afford any more children. Robin wanted a divorce but decided, since she loved babies so much, she would study midwifery. Now this is her profession, and she appears happy tending her brood of chicks as she delivers broods of other mothers' chicks into the world. Sonya, the least attractive of Dee's friends, is a skinny, shapeless thing with the pasty complexion of a corpse. She'd never been in the presence of a male until her first job on Capitol Hill, where she met Rex Milsap. He is as skinny and shapeless as her, and his face is pockmarked from a teenage war with acne. Now with their bespeckled, knobby-kneed, nerdy offspring and their like-minded policy wonk personalities, they couldn't seem happier. Kathy too, even though she's been divorced, seems happy. She dispensed with her neglectful husband in favor of an attentive one. Not that Dee minds attention, but not too much of the negative kind. She assumes that is the kind Gail shoulders. Gail attended Denver University through her sophomore year, and then she scurried home with her tail between her legs after getting herself pregnant. She chased Ed Strickland around until he agreed to marry her—a hasty decision, considering the personality of her spouse. She can't imagine that Gail is happy. Not that happiness is that essential. Peace of mind is. Love is. It's worth waiting for both, and that's what she thought she might have found in Mitch Lovett before the bastard kicked the foundation from under her.

Dee is playing with her mixed field greens when the main course is served. She is not very hungry and ordered only another starter, the lobster salad with fried green tomato and goat cheese. Her other friends did the same, except for Sonya and Gail. Sonya ordered the burger and fries and Gail the hanger steak and root vegetables.

"I've read that hanger steak has fewer calories and cholesterol than chicken," Gail says. She and Sonya are prodigious eaters and thin as well, though Gail's figure, unlike Sonya's, is well defined, even attractive to some men who like the athletic type.

She's a blond like Dee. Dee checks out her old friend critically. Could she be the one? She can certainly imagine Gail's desire to cheat on Ed. She can't imagine Mitch's preference for Gail, especially after their all-night foray at her condo, but it is possible. Anything is possible. He could be having an affair with Sonya, who is also a blond, though a washed-out, dirty one. Finally, Dee cannot stand it any longer and grabs Kathy by the arm. She whispers between her teeth, "Let's go to the bathroom."

"Okay," says Kathy, sliding out of the booth after her.

Dee locks the door in the bathroom and leans against the sink.

"I have something to tell you that I want you to keep secret. You promise?"

Kathy closes the toilet seat and sits down. "I promise." She crosses her heart.

Dee takes a deep breath. "That wasn't me that Mitch was kissing in front of his house."

"Then who was it?"

"I don't know. But I was wondering—do you think it could be Gail?" asks Dee. She takes another deep breath.

"Oh, I doubt that. Even though Ed's a jerk, I doubt that she would go that far. After all, they have a kid—Gail is an excellent mother, and I don't think she would do anything that rash. If Ed found out, he could take Davy away from her. I don't think she could handle that."

"Yeah, that makes sense," says Dee, thinking that it doesn't matter who the blond was anyway. She won't let Mitch go without a fight.

Kathy laughs. "Don't worry," she says. "Mitch is a stable guy. I think he's over the divorce, and I'm not sure he wants to commit himself to anyone right now. There'll come a day when he's ready to settle down."

"I don't know if I'm willing to wait that long," says Dee.

When they return to the table, the ladies are on the subject of husbands. Sonya points out that her work for a congressman sometimes keeps her out late, especially during the election cycle, and there is always a struggle between her and Rex as far as childcare is concerned. Rex works for the World Bank and travels a fair amount.

"Sometimes I can't handle it, all the time he is gone—it makes me feel like a single parent."

"Maybe one of you should put your career on hold like I did," says Gail. She reminds them of her job with a high-end antique dealer in Georgetown, which she held until Davy was born. "I mean, it broke my heart to quit, but I didn't want my son to be raised by a stranger."

"I feel the same way," says Sonya. "But, you know, Rex and I will work it out."

"I know you will," says Robin, smiling in an officious way. "Barry and I did."

The dinner breaks up. They head out to the sidewalk in front of Republic and hug each other good night. But then Dee wanders back into the restaurant and sits down at the stainless steel bar, feeling upset. It's not only Mitch. She feels like she's drifting apart from her friends—or maybe it's more. She's not sure.

"What's your best drink?" she asks the bartender. He is a cute, bulgy-muscled guy—shaved head, gold earring, long golden beard, and the prettiest pale blue eyes that sparkle from the beaded lights above the bar.

He rubs his chin thoughtfully, "I would say an old fashioned if you select the best bourbon or rye." He points them out: Old Scout, Whistle Pig, Catoctin Creek, Filibuster, High West Rendezvous, and Buffalo Trace.

"Colorful names," she says, smiling at the fellow. "You pick one out."

He pulls down the High West. She watches as he mixes the drink and tells her that the secret to a great old fashioned is to go light on the sugar and bitters so that you don't overpower the flavor of the whiskey.

He slides the drink over to her. She takes a sip. "Oh, that's delicious," she says, feeling slightly tipsy. This is her second drink. The first one, the Fascist Killer, one of the restaurant's specialties, was equally potent.

The bartender smiles and strokes his long golden beard as he wanders off to another customer. Maybe she should shack up with this fellow. Cut off his beard. Just like Delilah. She could do it, she imagines, even though he's half her age.

She checks the other customers at the bar—all spring chickens except for the fellow next to her, who must be in his mid-fifties. He has blue eyes and thick glasses, but she doesn't notice much else, other than his stubby fingers around a beer bottle. "What's your name, honey?" he asks her when their eyes meet.

"Chicken Little," she says, feeling uneasy.

He laughs, licks his lips. "Okay, tell me Chicken Little, is the sky falling?"

She's about to tell the creep to get lost when the bartender rescues her. He points at her empty glass. "Want another?"

"No, thanks," she says, "think I'll cash in." She hands over her credit card, and when the bartender returns with the receipt, she considers writing her phone number down below her signature but decides not to. Life is complicated enough.

She hurries out to the street. It is mostly empty except for a bus, a couple of cabs, and a car full of teenagers. There are a few worker bees trudging up from the subway. She stops at the 7-Eleven, buys a pack of American Spirits, takes out one, and stuffs the rest in her purse. She lights the cigarette and draws in the smoke. She hasn't indulged in what, ten years, but feels so down in the dumps. Why not? By the time she reaches the Metro station, she is so dizzy she has to lean against a post until the train arrives.

On the way home, Dee watches the reflection of her face in the window. It is a dark night behind the glass; a few streetlights and the headlights from cars along the track streak by. She must decide what to do. When the train enters the tunnel at Union Station, she feels an overwhelming gloom that makes her body shiver. She feels so jealous of her friends. Somehow she never did before. Before, she thought she had a life. Before, she had the job, the accolades, the money, the late-night confabs at local bars after work, the parties and conventions. Sometimes she'd come home alone. Sometimes she'd come home with a man. He'd spend the night or not, depending on her whims. Sometimes the sparks would fly. Sometimes she would develop a relationship with a man that ran its course at the speed of light, so fast that, afterward, she could hardly remember the man and why she had been in love with him. Her longest relationship was with Jack Tucker. It was hard to avoid him. They worked in the same office. The thing about Jack is that he wanted to be in bed with her all the time, maybe because when they weren't in bed, they fought. The only thing that would stop the fighting was when he thought he could get in bed with her again. Then he'd give her little gifts, bawdy Valentines, red panties with split crotches. Jack Fucker, she called him behind his back—way too high maintenance.

One of her colleagues, a woman of fifty who is now in Dubai—her firm is international—told Dee that men are worthless. This woman was pregnant when she was eighteen. Her boyfriend left her when she was twenty. "I've been alone ever since," she said, "raising a child. I've been happy as a clam."

Maybe that's what she wants, a child—not Mitch Lovett. But then she remembers her promise to herself. In a couple weeks, she'll visit her mom. Her house backs up on Opal Daniels Park, where the Stork Club is having a picnic. Maybe she'll show up there. If Mitch comes, maybe she'll find the blond and figure out what to do next.

Chapter Five

Mitch is sitting in the living room of the Woodland house waiting to pick up Addie and Julian for an overnight at the Crowne Plaza. He stares at a black-and-white illustration on the wall next to the fireplace, which he inherited from his father. It is of a dapper gentleman, a black cape draped over his shoulder, black top hat tilted jauntily on his head. He wears a white mask and gloves. He carries a cane in one hand and lights a cigarette with the other. It's an ad for a tobacco shop in New Orleans—the model for the illustration was his father, the illustrator his mother. Her name is on the bottom right-hand corner below the shoe. Teresa Lovett. Mitch used to whisper her name under his breath: Teresa Lovett. Teresa Lovett. He missed his mother even though he never remembered much about her, other than, as his father told him, she was a good Catholic. He doesn't care for religion.

He remembers his father's other women. Some were nice to him, some not so much. One locked him in the closet because his dad didn't give her enough attention. She needn't bother.

Kathy tiptoes in from the kitchen balancing a tea set and a plate of cookies on a silver tray. She sets the tray down on the mission-style coffee table, pours a cup for Mitch and another for herself. She hands him the plate. He takes a cookie. Salted oatmeal again. "To what do I owe this honor?" he asks, knowing that she has something up her sleeve and it's not pleasant, because otherwise she would reveal it right away. He supposes she is about to launch into one of her analyses. She is not a Freudian exactly, but she puts a lot of store in the past.

So he decides that he will help her out. He wanders over to the illustration hanging from the wall next to the fireplace and stares at his mother's name. "You know, I forget to take this drawing when I moved out," he says, munching the cookie.

"I thought you did that on purpose."

"No, I forgot it. Can I have it now?"

"Sure. Why not? It's yours."

He takes down the illustration and puts it on the coffee table where he won't forget it.

"Do you remember when we went to Mardi Gras when the kids were little? You dragged me to the Garden District so you could show me the little yellow house where you spent the first three years of your life. Only it was blue," says Kathy, tapping her glasses against her teeth in a thoughtful manner.

"You told me the only memory you have of your mother is that once you were in the backyard playing with a lawn mower. The handle fell back and conked you in the head. You raised a ruckus, and your mom raced over and gathered you in her arms. You don't recall much other than the color of her hair—I forget what it is..."

"Same as yours."

"...and that she smelled good."

"Could've been the flowers. We had a beautiful garden." He reaches out for another cookie but thinks better of it. "Where's Bob?"

"He'll be here soon," she says with a wave of her hand. "Tell me something. Do you hate women?"

"Oh, that again," he says. Whenever she was ticked off at him, she'd ask him that question. She thought that he must feel abandoned. First his mother abandoned him, though it wasn't her fault (she died of breast cancer). Then all those other women—it seemed there was a different lady every week unless his dad married one. Then they'd hang out for a couple of years before his father would show them the door. Maybe she thought he hated women when actually he hated his father. *There's a psychological term for that,* he remembers. Displacement.

"You want to be analytical about it," he says, leaning closer. She puts on her red-framed glasses to scrutinize him more closely. She has three pairs, red, green, and yellow— stoplights, one of her patients calls them. Even with all the water under the bridge, he still loves her. "My only memory of my mother is when she came to my rescue to ease my pain. That means that I must not hate women."

"So it's the pain that's bothering you," says Kathy, smiling knowingly and tapping her glasses against her chin. "You think women are a salve to ease your pain?"

"I don't think that at all," he says, smiling back. "However, I think women are sometimes the cause of the pain."

"So it's all right to jump from woman to woman? Because one woman caused the pain, you try to ease it with another?" Now she puts on her reading glasses, the yellow ones, and leans even closer, as if she's inspecting the pores in his skin. "Have you ever thought about anyone but yourself? Have you thought about Dee and her feelings? She may want a serious relationship and, from what I can tell, you don't. So why string her along?"

Mitch looks down at his hands and shrugs.

But before she can enlighten him further, Bob shuffles in the front door followed by Julian and Addie who race up to their daddy, all excited, and hug him tightly.

Addie says, "I love you, Daddy."

"I love you, darling," says Mitch, "and you too, Julian."

The kids clomp upstairs to pack for their overnight. Bob shakes Mitch's hand. His hands are clammy. He looks beat. "Those two are a handful," he says before he follows them up to their bedrooms.

"He doesn't have the stamina you have," says Kathy, sighing.

"He's all brain, and I'm all brawn," says Mitch scrutinizing his ex as intensely as she scrutinizes him. "But enough of this. Let's get down to brass tacks. What are you getting at with how I'm stringing Dee along and this psychological analysis about how I hate woman, or whatever?"

"Well, okay," Kathy says, grimacing. "What I'm trying to get at is that Bull saw you the other night outside your house kissing a woman, and I know it wasn't Dee because she told me later that she'd never been at your house on Oak Lane."

"Do you want me to tell you who it was?" asks Mitch. He looks down at his hands again as if they hold the answer.

"No, I don't want to know," she says in a loud whisper because the kids are clomping down the stairs lugging their stuff. "It's none of my business if you run around Takoma Park with all your hurt feelings. But the kids are my business. Don't do anything that reflects poorly on them."

"Don't worry," he whispers, leaning close to his ex, "the kids are my business, too."

Mitch drives Addie and Julian to White Flint Mall to see a movie. But it's *Snow White* and they already have the CD.

"I'm sorry."

"It's not your fault," says Julian. "How would you know? You don't even live with us anymore."

Addie drags him to the Discovery Zone. He hates the place, his vision of hell. The walls and ceilings are painted in bright, happy colors. The kids scurry about, screeching like a horde of mice frightened by a hungry cat. He hands the money to a cashier. Addie and Julian dart past Mitch. Almost knock him over. They vanish in the playground, a huge, multilevel maze made of sturdy, bright-colored plastic and netting, guarded by teenage helpers who seem as overwhelmed as he is.

Mitch stations himself at the entrance, the only means of escape. He waits forever. Ten minutes. Twenty minutes. Half an hour until he sees Addie slip headfirst down a slide. She wants something to drink. They head for the concession, his eyes still on the playground, watching for Julian. He purchases two lemonades. They sit down. Addie gabs about the trouble that Julian's in at summer camp.

"The coach made him sit in the corner for twenty minutes."

"You're kidding."

"Yeah, he hit a kid in the back of the head with a soccer ball. The kid bit his lip and bled all over his shirt."

"Did he throw the ball on purpose?"

"He kicked the ball," she says. "He meant to kick it."

Julian climbs down a rope ladder, looks for his father.

Mitch waves at him. He waves back, turns, and jumps in a bin of multicolored plastic balls.

"You know what else he did? The lady in the computer class made him stand in the corner for five minutes because he talked about toilets."

"You mean toilet talk."

"Yeah. What's toilet talk?" she asks.

Mitch watches Julian and another boy throw plastic balls at each other in the bin. One of the balls bounces off the boy's head. He screeches like a demon. Mitch grabs Addie's hand and drags her over to Julian, but, by the time he gets there, he's gone. The boy screeches louder in a voice that sounds like chalk scrapped across a blackboard. Mitch tries to sooth the boy.

Addie yells, "What's toilet talk?"

Mitch reaches over to help the boy out of the bin. He stops crying, eyes on someone behind him. A bantamweight man, bald eagle tattoo on his arm, grabs the boy by the hand and hurries off.

"I have to go to the bathroom," exclaims Addie.

"You can't," says Mitch, "until we find Julian."

They wait another ten minutes. The whole time, Addie crosses her legs, bends forward, saying, "Please, Daddy. Please, Daddy."

When Mitch sees Julian, he grabs his hand and they're off to the bathroom.

They wait outside for an impossible amount of time. Addie's as bad as her mother.

"I hear you're in trouble in camp," says Mitch.

Julian crosses his arms and pouts. "Did Addie tell you that?" he asks. "That rat."

"Now, Julian, it doesn't matter who told me," Mitch says, bending down until his eyes are at the same level as his son's. "I don't like toilet talk, and I don't like it when you hit someone in the head with a ball."

"I didn't hit him on the head on purpose."

"I suppose you didn't hit the boy in the head with a ball over there"—he points at the bin full of balls—"and make him cry."

"Yes, I did. But he was throwing balls at me too."

Addie skips out, a wet spot in front of her dress where she spilled some water when she washed up. Mitch tries to clean her up, and while he does, Julian vanishes. Mitch panics for a moment until he thinks he sees his son crawl past a window in a long, fuchsia tube on the second level of the playground. He tells Addie to find him. He rushes out to the mall, his eyes still on the entrance to the Discovery Zone. He glances up and down the walkway. No Julian.

One time, when he was married, Kathy got mad at him for walking ahead of the kids in the mall. You've got to keep your eyes on them, she said. She told him the story of Adam Walsh, the kid who was snatched from a mall when his mother turned away for a moment. They found his head later in a canal, but never his body. Mitch thought he was being talked down to. He scuttled sideways, crab-like. See I'm watching them, he said, but he actually took what she said to heart. He knew the chances of Julian being snatched were one in a million, but he didn't want to be that one, and that's what he feels like now, as he moves over to guard the Discovery Zone entrance, a lump in his throat, defying all reason.

Ten minutes pass. Then, at twenty, Addie emerges from the bin full of plastic balls, followed by Julian. Mitch drags them to the men's room and slings them into the stall, as much for safekeeping as to keep Addie from witnessing anything unsavory at the urinals. He goes to the bathroom. He hears an ominous sound from the stall behind him and, in his haste, zips up some skin. Yelps. Dances around on one leg until the pain subsides. He bangs on the locked door.

"Open up."

"I'm trying, Dad," says Julian.

Mitch waits an endless time until the door flies open. Addie stands in a pool of unraveled toilet paper.

"Did you do that?"

"We both did that, Dad," says Julian. Both kids smile sheepishly at their dad.

"Come on." He takes them to McDonalds, where he lectures Julian about disappearing, a mild version of the Adam Walsh story. Julian has heard this story before, maybe a thousand times, but he does not seem bored. He wants to know why anyone would snatch a kid. What do they do with a kid? He's asked these questions before, and as before he's not satisfied with the answers. He wants specifics.

"I'm sorry, Julian, I'll tell you more when you're older."

"That's what you always say," he groans. Crosses his arms. Pouts again.

"Eat your lunch," says Mitch.

"I'm not hungry."

"I've got to go to the bathroom," whines Addie.

"Go ahead."

"What if the snatcher's in there?"

"There's no one in there but other girls and women."

"Wait by the door for me. Will you please, Daddy?" She takes his hand and holds it to her face pleadingly.

"Okay." He takes her to the bathroom, which is in sight of the table where Julian is sitting.

Barry Spicer ambles past him with a tray full of a salad, large fries, large hamburger, large Coke, and apple turnover. He pauses at the table where Julian's is sitting. Says something to him, sits down, and waves at Mitch.

When Mitch and Addie get back to the table, Barry says, "Isn't this a surprise. What are you doing in my territory?" He takes a half-moon out of his hamburger.

"We're on an overnight at the Crowne Plaza." The kids stare up at Barry in quiet amazement as he polishes off the hamburger in two more bites. He licks his fingertips and grabs a fistful of fries.

"Hey, Daddy, remember that comic book you read to us the last time we were at the hotel?" says Addie.

"Popeye."

"Yeah, Mr. Spicer is like that guy who ate hamburgers."

"Wimpy," says Julian.

"Yeah."

Barry scowls at the kids. Changes the subject quickly. "You should check out the new Saabs," he says as he slaps the salt off his hands. He grabs another fistful of fries. "The design's completely changed, back to the old Saab lines, and the engine too—there's a V-6 on the market now. Cheaper. Pickup matches the turbo model."

"Great," says Mitch.

"Listen, you have one of the old nine-hundreds—a great car, but it lacks the punch of the new one," says Barry. "You need to come down and see us. I'll be there all day." He finishes up his fries, slaps his hands, and digs into the salad.

"Later," says Mitch, "when I'm not with the kids."

"Sure. Sure. I understand," Barry says, playing with his salad. He's dressed in a pinstriped suit. A monogrammed handkerchief sticks out of the breast pocket. He pokes Mitch in the side. "Hey, you know what Bull told me a couple of nights ago?"

"You mean about Dee," says Mitch. "Yeah, I know. From Kathy."

"Darn. News travels like wildfire." Barry laughs. "But Bull didn't say it was Dee. He said it was a blond woman that could've been Dee, but he didn't think so because she wasn't heavy enough up top."

"It was Dee," insists Mitch.

"Oh, yeah," says Barry, smiling wryly as if he was playing along with the lie. "That's great. You and Dee make a great couple." He grabs the apple turnover, still in its wrapper. Sticks it in his pocket. Stands up. "Got to hustle back to the office."

After Barry disappears down an escalator, Julian tugs at his father's sleeve. "I don't want to go to the haunted house tonight. I'm afraid of ghosts."

"We're going to the Crowne Plaza," says Mitch.

"Yippee, yippee, yippee," says Julian as he jumps out his chair and skips around the table. "Can we play miniature golf?"

"Yes, we can," says his father, laughing at his son's antics.

Addie imitates her brother. "I'm playing miniature golf. I'm playing miniature golf," she sings, looking up at her father for approval.

They drive to the divorced dad's hangout, a seven-story building, open on a central court that includes a bar, a restaurant, the golf course, and a three-story waterfall that trickles down a fake stone bed to a pool next to a lounge area with a big-screen TV.

It's an ideal hangout for the dads because they can sit at the elevated bar where they can see their kids play golf or blitz out on TV. Mitch doesn't like the place. He won't go up to the bar because all the men are doing is complaining about their former wives. Their unfair divorce settlements. Visitation rights. The cramped apartments they live in. He plays a round of golf with Addie and Julian. They are having a great time, and this makes Mitch happy.

After dinner, they head upstairs. The kids turn on the television. Julian wants to stay up all night.

"You can stay up until ten," says Mitch.

Addie runs through the channels until she comes to the pay TV channel where they're doing a preview of *Snow White.*

"I want to see it," she screams.

"You can't. You can't," her brother screams back.

"Hold on," says Mitch. "Now, Addie, you had your chance to see Snow White at the movies today, but you wanted to go to Discovery Zone because you had the movie at home. Do you have the movie at home?"

"Yes."

"Then you can see it at home."

"I want to see it here," she says in her tiny, endearing voice. She starts to blubber.

"I'm sorry, honey, but Julian may want to watch something else."

"Cartoons," says Julian.

Addie breaks out into full-fledged sobs until she hears her father's voice again.

"Maybe we can watch *Snow White* if we can convince your brother."

"Never." Julian crosses his arms over his chest. Insists that he wants cartoons.

Addie sobs loudly.

Mitch switches the channels until he comes to a cartoon version of Winnie the Pooh.

"You like Winnie the Pooh, don't you, darling?" he asks his daughter.

Addie stops sobbing and stares at the screen. "Yes."

"You do too, Julian."

"Yeah. Sure." He climbs on the bed and lies on his stomach. Addie climbs up beside him.

"You can stay up until ten," he says, but they are asleep in five minutes.

Mitch lies back in the bed to stare at the ceiling and think about Gail Strickland. She is camping with her husband tonight in White Oak Canyon in the Blue Ridge Mountains. She would rather be here, she told Mitch when they met again at his house after their first foray into lovemaking. They made love again and twice more after that. It was beginning to remind him of when he met Kathy—they couldn't restrain themselves. He turns over on his side and tries to fall asleep, but he is thinking about what is transpiring out there as if it was Ed, not he, who is the transgressor. But that will soon change if Gail does what she promised.

Chapter Six

Gail and Ed Strickland hike down White Oak Canyon trail, following the creek. When they come to the waterfalls, the trail grows steeper until, at the bottom, Gail collapses on her backpack, sweaty and exhausted. The sky is barely visible through the trees. Shafts of light poke through holes in the leafy canopy. The largest shaft of light lands on the pool at the bottom of a thirty-foot waterfall.

Ed reaches in his backpack and pulls out a bottle of Dr. Bonner's soap. "You clean yourself off while I pitch the tent."

Gail strips down to her underwear and jumps in the pool. It is freezing cold. Tiny fishes nibble at her toes, but it doesn't bother her. She swims under the waterfall. The water splashes her head and shoulders. Her skin tingles, and she relaxes. When she swims back, Ed is sitting on a rock removing his clothes. He grabs the Dr. Bonner's and jumps in the water.

"Cold," he says as he squirts some of the soap in his hand and rubs it over her back and shoulders. He removes her bra, tosses it on shore, and runs his slick hands over her breasts.

"Aren't you afraid someone will hike down the trail and see us?" she asks in a soft voice.

"There was only one car in the parking lot and those people hiked by us." He turns her hand over and squirts some Dr. Bonner in it. "Why don't you jack me off?"

"Why do you have to use such crude language?"

"Ah, jeez, I'm about to leave for the convention in Salt Lake City. I won't see you for, I don't know, five days. Can't a man have any pleasure," he says, pushing her hand underwater. She jacks him off, though it's difficult. He leans against a rock and she has to admit he looks beautiful with his athletic build and all, but she feels not an ounce of desire for him.

They climb out of the pool and step in their clothes. They build a fire and heat their dinner, dehydrated vegetables and tuna in a can, with Twinkies for dessert and a cup of tea with a whiskey chaser. They clean up the dishes, pile more wood on the fire, and stare at the flames until it's dark. Ed wants to make love.

They duck into the tent and he humps her twice, groaning and grunting, as if he was Sisyphus pushing a rock up a hill.

"What's the matter? You didn't make any noise," he asks her after rolling off her the second time. "Didn't you enjoy it?"

"I enjoyed it. It was wonderful," she lies. The truth is that Ed cares only for himself. Early on in their marriage she gave him a book titled *She Comes First*. She thought even if he didn't crack the book open—he hated to read—the title itself would give him an idea of how to approach sex with a woman. But no, he threw the book in the trash and didn't speak to her for two days. She might as well be a pillow.

Ed falls asleep, content, mumbling to himself. Gail turns away from him. The ground is hard. She feels a sharp object beneath her hip and digs it out of the ground, smoothing out the space it leaves. It's a small twig with a sharp end. She tosses it out of the tent. Ed wakes up, turns on his side toward her, and curls his hand around her breast.

"What's up? What's up?" He smacks his lips. She lies totally still, hoping he will fall back to sleep. He does. The grip on her breast loosens. She removes his hand and pushes him gently to his side of the tent. He lets go with a hissing sigh that sounds like air escaping a tire.

She curls her hands under her chin but can't fall asleep. Now she is distracted by the racket outside the tent, the water pounding against the rocks in the pool, an army of crickets banging away like drummers in the dark African night in a Tarzan movie. Worse. Ed is like a living, breathing, malevolent version of the King of the Apes, one who wants to harm her—and, if she as much as breathes a word about her wish to divorce him, as she promised Mitch, she has no doubt he would strangle her to death and some lonely hiker would find her in a couple of weeks, tossed into the woods like a rag doll. *Men,* she thinks. Somehow, Ed convinced himself that she would prefer this primeval setting to a bed and breakfast because they could conjoin here like the crickets in the trees and she would be satisfied, which she probably would if she was a figment of male fantasy like Tarzan's Jane. Gail giggles to herself.

Ed wakes up. "What's up? What's up?" He smacks his lips again.

"Nothing is up, darling," she says in a soothing voice. "Go back to sleep."

He smacks his lips again. Sighs and soon is making tiny gasping sounds, his attempt at snoring.

She lays on her side, still unable to sleep, and inventories all the years gone by. Thinks about how they sailed through their first two years of marriage, if not in love then at least close to each other. She knew when he wanted to talk or when to sit there quietly with him, holding hands, or when to totally back off. She didn't exactly like that he was moody, but she kept that in the back of her mind. What was foremost was the growing familiarity, the feel of his lean, muscular body, the sweet citrus smell of his skin, and the sound of his voice, how it sometimes cracked when he got excited. How he laughed out of the side of his mouth like a gangster. She liked this. She could see that things could work out in a positive way even though sometimes he lost his temper. Back then, he took it out on inanimate objects. Chairs. Walls. She began thinking about starting a family. She wanted to put what happened to her in Colorado behind her. But she should have known better. In the fall of their fourth year of marriage the Montgomery Blair football team lost their first game twenty-one to nothing. Ed was the offensive coordinator; Ed's father and the head coach blamed him. Too many dropped passes. Too many fumbles. Too many botched plays.

That day, she waited for Ed in the car. He came out. Slammed the door as he got in. He didn't lean over to kiss her as he usually did. She could see by his smoldering eyes, the petulant look on his face, that he was like a volcano about to erupt. Gail kept quiet.

They drove home. Climbed the stairs to their apartment, the second floor of a house on Wayne Avenue. Ate dinner. She could hear the clinking of utensils against dishware, but that's it. Finally, she could no longer stand it.

"There'll be other games," she said.

Ed gave her a sullen, lopsided grin, stood up, and socked her in the shoulder with such force that she toppled backward in the chair. Hit her head on the floor. She saw stars. It didn't seem to hurt that much, though she wobbled to her feet, holding on to the kitchen counter until her head cleared. She turned slowly, afraid Ed was going to attack again.

He stood at the head of the table, his fists balled, a disdainful snarl on his lips, but in his eyes she could see a look of concern. She knew that the concern was not for her and this made her furious at the bastard though she didn't say a word. She sidled into the bathroom. Cleaned herself off, her hands shaking. She changed her clothes and headed to the front door to the apartment. She put her hand on the doorknob but didn't twist it. She turned.

"Don't you even care that you hurt me?" she asked.

He was in the same position only the snarl had gone from his lips and his eyes were focused on her with what seemed like regret. "Sure, I care," he said.

But he didn't come to her. He didn't say he was sorry. Maybe it was pride that stopped him. She didn't care. She twisted the knob, opened the door, and walked out.

Gail spent the night in a motel in Silver Spring, unable to sleep. Next door she heard a drunk slurring his words and a woman's voice. She couldn't tell if the voice came from a television—there was dramatic music in the background. If the woman was real, perhaps she was a hooker. It was that type of motel. Gail tested the bruise on her shoulder, which had turned a nasty purple, and the lump on the back of her head. Is there something that she did to deserve to get beat up? To hide out in a cheap motel like a criminal? She entertained the thought of leaving Ed.

But this thought was polluted by the night, the sirens that wailed outside her window, the groaning noise in the next room, the sound of footsteps in the hallway. At 3:00 a.m., someone banged on her door. At first she thought it was Ed, and she was all excited that he had worked so hard to find her. But it was the drunk. She told him to go away.

Gail hears a tree limb snap outside the tent, maybe a human being invading their camp, or Sasquatch, but more likely a raccoon. She opens the tent flap and peers out. She hears a chattering sound and then catches a squirrel outlined by the embers of their fire dragging a stick loaded with acorns to the woods. Gail falls back in bed and thinks about how she felt back then, in that motel in Silver Spring. Not much different than she feels now. Bad. So bad it made her want to do something, so she went into the bathroom, filled the tub, and took off all her clothes. She climbed into the tub and thought about suicide. How wonderful it would be if she had a razor. She'd lay back enshrouded by the silky, hot softness of the water. She would slit her wrists with the razor, lengthwise along the path of her veins so the blood would flow quickly. She would keep her arms buried under water. She would close her eyes and drift into a dreamless sleep.

She wondered, what would it be like to be dead? To be in a place where no man could touch her, punch her, kiss her, and screw her. Where she couldn't have children. Feel the pain of losing one or the pleasure that might come if she didn't lose one, the pleasure of pushing her baby down the street in a baby carriage on a beautiful, spring day. If she couldn't have a baby, would the beautiful spring day be pleasure enough? Or would she prefer the void, a total absence of light, feeling, and consciousness? No pain. No pleasure. No heaven. No hell. Nothing. A big bunch of nothing—that's the way she imagined eternity, a bunch of nothing where nothing ever happened.

Finally, she had enough of this kind of thinking. Climbed out of the tub. Felt the cold air meet her body. Raise goose bumps on her skin. She wrapped herself in a towel. Turned on the hair dryer. Felt the warm air on her scalp. Looked at her hair flying wildly in the mirror over the bathroom sink. She dried the rest of her body off and slipped back into her clothes. She climbed back in bed and checked the clock: 5:00 a.m. She called Ed. He hustled over immediately, strolled into the room, and handed her twelve red roses. Where was he able to pick them up that time of morning? She wondered. He sat on the bed. Held her hand.

"I'm a horrible person," he confessed. "I let my emotions get the best of me, when I know, logically, that losing a football game doesn't matter. It doesn't matter that the coach blames me. Even Dad. If I was fired on the spot, that doesn't matter. I can find another job. What matters is how I treat you because, you know, if I treat you badly and you leave me, where would I turn?"

For two weeks after Ed's assault, Gail suffered from headaches and dizziness. She went to a doctor. He told her she had a concussion. He noticed the bruise on her shoulder and asked her where she got it from. Did it have anything to do with the concussion? She said it didn't. She left the office and didn't come back. That was a stupid mistake. She should've told the doctor. Instead, she had a baby, and Ed calmed down for a time and went back to attacking inanimate objects. Once, she remembers, he attacked the wall when he wanted to attack her. He sprained his wrist. It was almost comical, the way he tried to keep himself under control, but lately she didn't see it as comical or anything else. She didn't care.

Gail reaches behind her head and feels the knot. She thinks about Mitch. He said at their last meeting that he loved her. He didn't say, "I love you, and you ought to get divorced." She came up with that idea. He did not object. He smiled in a secretive way, as if this was what he wanted most of all.

The next morning, Gail and Ed hike the rest of the way down White Oak Canyon and follow the trail that winds up Old Rag Mountain, a rocky peak on the eastern slope of the Blue Ridge. They leave their gear at the shelter and hike down a trail to a spring where they fill their canteens. They sit down to watch the sunset.

"Remember how, before we married, my parents threw us a camping shower," says Ed, pulling her toward him. "And we received gifts like the huge clunky boots that looked like something Frankenstein would wear and the Coleman stove that weighed thirty pounds and two down sleeping bags that would've worked in Alaska but not around here?"

"We returned those things," says Gail, watching the sun sink behind the trees.

"Yes, we did and then we never went camping except that one time when we were in the Smoky Mountains on our honeymoon. I pitched a tent while you waited in the car because it was drizzling out."

"And there was thunder and lightning, and then the wind picked up, blowing the tent against you so you couldn't stake it down, and I insisted that we find some place decent to stay."

"That motel on the lake with the feather bed. We watched *Show Boat* on the TV, and I looked out the window to see if the weather cleared, but all I could see was the lightning flashes in the mountains. Even I wasn't willing to go out in that."

"But you were cranky the whole time in a cute way that didn't bother me," she says remembering how she felt in the past. "Even when you threw a little fit when the movie was over because I insisted I was too tired to make love."

"Yeah, those were good times," says Ed, squeezing her hand. "We made love the next morning in that feather bed though I don't see how we managed it the way our bodies kept sinking deeper and deeper. I thought we'd drown."

"I really cared for you," says Gail, watching a large bird, probably a hawk, dive-bomb a smaller one at the treetops and chase it over the ridge to the other side of the mountain.

"Does that mean you don't care for me now?"

"I didn't say that."

"Well, you don't enjoy a lot of things I enjoy, like camping."

"I know I don't enjoy the outdoors like you do, but I do try," she says. "You remember the time I went deer hunting in western Pennsylvania with you and Bull? We followed the trail of a deer you wounded until we came to a field, and there it was lying on the ground, its tongue hanging out, gasping for breath."

"You didn't like that."

"No, and I didn't like the other time we went hunting, near Rehoboth Beach, when I spent the whole day frozen to death in a duck blind waiting for ducks that never showed up."

"And the nights at the Atlantic Sand Motel. You had a good time, as I remember it," says Ed, taking his arm from around her shoulder and moving away from her slightly.

"I was three months pregnant."

"What does that have to do with it?"

"Nothing," she says, trying to gain some courage, "except sometimes I wish you showed some concern for me."

He looks at her sharply. She can tell that he is angry by the way his eyes narrow. "I do show concern. I've taken care of you ever since we've been married. Even though I don't like my job, I've gone every day."

That was a lie. He'd gone every day because he loved his job. The only time he didn't love it was when Blair lost a game.

"Hey, I know you work hard and it's been frustrating at times," she says softly, trying to appease him, "but that's the way life is. It's not easy."

"What are you, a philosopher?" he growls. "We were having this nice, pleasant conversation, and you have to change the subject."

"I wasn't trying to change the subject, exactly, though I think maybe it's good idea we talk about our relationship. That's all," she says, though she doesn't mean it. It's beyond talking as far as she's concerned.

"Is that why you came out here, so we could talk about our relationship?" he asks, standing up, folding his arms across his chest, and staring down at her. "Isn't it enough to be with your husband?"

"Yes, it is," she says deciding that it is useless to pursue this further.

"Good. Good," he says, eyeing her carefully. "You don't want to leave me?"

"No, I don't," she says quickly.

"I don't think I could stand it if you left me."

"You have nothing to worry about."

He reaches down and runs his hand through her hair. He smiles. "Okay. Okay," he says. He seems satisfied. "I think what I'll do now is hunt for some wood. We'll put a fire together and cook dinner."

Ed picks up the canteens, slings them over his shoulder. Reaches down with his other hand, which Gail takes. He yanks her up to her feet, and they walk back to the campsite.

Chapter Seven

Dee Wynn wakes up with a headache at her mom's house on Sherman Avenue and crawls to the bathroom. She pops three Advils. Lies down for ten minutes until her head clears. She combs her hair in front of the vanity mirror and looks out the window at Opal Daniels Park. The Stork Club will meet for their picnic in four hours. Normally, she would stay away from the little brats and their overly indulgent parents (even if they are her friends), but this is a special occasion. She is determined to find out the identity of this blond woman that Mitch kissed in front of his house, and whether she is a serious contender or a dalliance, as Kathy contends.

Dee drags herself downstairs to the kitchen, where her mother, the good doctor, is fixing breakfast, a cup of tea, toast, and half a grapefruit for herself.

"What do you want?" she asks. "I could make you bacon. Eggs. Oatmeal. You want coffee?"

"Yes, and oatmeal, Mom."

"You're watching your weight. That's good." Dr. Wynn pats her daughter's hand.

Since her father's death, her mother's buried herself in her practice. Even at night, if Dee wants to reach her, she calls the office. There's solace in work, she says.

"Do you have any new prospects?" she asks her daughter.

"No, Mom, I have no new prospects."

"Weren't you thinking of going out with Kathy's old husband?"

"Yes, Mom."

"I don't know if I like that idea," she says. She twists her hair around her finger, which tells Dee that she's nervous, about to say something she deems important. "After all, Kathy's one of your dearest friends. I remember when you were confirmed at Little Flower in your pretty white dresses. You looked like twins. You've been inseparable ever since."

"Yes, Mom."

"I think you should do something like join a club where, you know, there'll be men around. Maybe you could take dance lessons. As a matter of fact, I'll join with you. We're both in the same situation."

"Mom."

"Well, all right, we're not in the same situation. You're still young enough to have children. All my children except you have children. I want you to have children too."

"Mom."

"Nothing in the world is more important than children. It's hard to explain until you've been through the experience. But raising children is the business of life."

"Mom. Please, quit with the platitudes."

"I'm sorry," Dr. Wynn says, shaking her head sadly and picking at her grapefruit. "I know it's not an easy thing, finding a man. I just want you to be happy."

"I have my work," Dee says in a tired voice.

"Do you think work makes you happy? Have you ever heard someone on their deathbed say, 'I wish I spent more time at the office'?"

"No, I haven't heard someone say that, but I have heard of many women who enjoy living without a man," she says, finally exasperated at her mother's hectoring. "Anyway, I am not one of those women. And for your information, I am going to marry Mitch Lovett."

Dr. Wynn drops her spoon. "Did I hear you correctly? What do you mean, you're going to marry Mitch? Did he propose to you?"

"No, Mom, but he will."

"Oh, I don't want to hurt your feelings, darling, but you should never expect anything from a recently divorced man," warns her mother in the same fashion Kathy had—though she seems to puzzle over it for a moment and taps her chin.

"Though I suppose nothing is impossible if you approach it in the right way."

Dr. Wynn heads off on a riff about how Gil, her departed spouse, asked her out on one date after another before they were married. She always declined until one day, she saw him at a movie with one of the leggy, blond nurses from the hospital where they were interns.

"He was ten years older than me. Returned from the war. That's why he was so far behind the rest of us. I didn't see him as marriage material at all. But when I saw him with that nurse, I was so jealous, the next time he asked me out, I accepted. He told me later that he had planned the whole thing." She laughed, wiped a tear from her eye. "He outwitted your poor mother."

Dee heads down the hill to Opal Daniels Park thinking now that she has one monkey off her back, she has to work on the other—though, at the same time, she wonders why. What is it with this knot in her stomach that she is feeling now? Is it doubt? Why is she pursuing her best friend's former husband? He does not have that much to recommend him, though he was once on a promising career path. First at CNN then freelancing. His work appeared on the National Geographic channel and public television. Since his divorce, though, he has become a man of leisure, working when he feels like it, filming advertisements for local businesses and such. But clearly, that does not challenge his intelligence. Maybe he could get involved in documentary film or features. She'll have to talk to him. Or is it even worth it? He lives in a dump. Kathy hinted that he is a shrewd businessman, that the dump might be an investment and that, besides, he has money stashed away. But who knows if that's true? Dee wants to continue living the good life. She doesn't want to take on a new burden.

So what is the attraction? It's physical, no doubt, but mental as well. She can see sadness in his hazel-colored eyes that she imagines only she can purge. She wants to dive into his head and swim around. See what makes him tick. He is a mystery, she thinks, as she approaches the park through the trees.

Just as she is about to emerge into the huge, grassy field that makes up most of the park, she sees Gail and Mitch beside a fence that shields them from the rest of the Stork Club members.

They're talking quietly. Dee only catches a few words, something about filming for the park service somewhere. A battlefield. Probably Civil War, she thinks, since there are so many around here. But she can't hear which one, nor when it will take place. Not that it matters, but it seems to animate Gail. She reaches out to touch Mitch, but he jumps back when he sees Dee.

"Hello," he says. "What a surprise? What are you doing here?"

"Maybe I should ask you the same question," says Dee, wondering again if Gail is the one. She's blond, but not a beauty and not that smart. She loves antiques, but big deal. Why would Mitch ever sleep with her, considering his alternatives?

"Oh, we're going to the Stork Club picnic," says Gail.

"Where's Ed?" Dee asks.

"He's at one of his sports conventions in Salt Lake City," says Gail, smiling insipidly.

"Oh, I see," says Dee, smiling back. "Well, I'm here because I was visiting my mom and I saw you guys so I thought I'd come down and say hello."

All three of them stroll across the field to the playground. The rest of the club is gathered around two picnic tables, where a vegetarian feast is spread out: Popeye pizzas, fruit, pasta, three bean salads, and a sheet cake that says *Stork Club Fifth Anniversary*. Next to the table is a cooler that contains apple juice, wine, and beer. The adults gorge themselves while the children run wild over the playground like mice chased by a cat. They shriek and jabber, but they do not bother Dee. Their voices don't carry. Chubby, baby Ralph, Robin's youngest, squirms in her arms. He munches contentedly on an Oreo cookie. The partially digested pieces are broadcast downwind and land unnoticed on his father's head. Barry is inhaling a pizza slice and talking to Mitch about Saabs.

"It's so nice to see you," Robin exclaims to Dee. She picks at the three-bean salad, and Ralph tries to grab her fork. "I don't think I've ever seen you at a Stork Club event before."

"I was visiting mom and I saw you guys down here," says Dee.

"So you came to pay your respects," says Robin.

"Yes, exactly."

"Not to check out Mitch," she says, narrowing her eyes as if she knows better.

"That too." They both stare at Mitch. He's fidgeting, half listening to Barry while watching Bob push Addie and Julian in a tire swing.

Dee excuses herself to wander toward Bob. Julian jumps off his swing and runs to her, staggering sideways when the tire hits him in the back. He jumps into her arms. "Auntie Dee," he screams. He plants kisses on her cheek, buries his face in her neck. She puts him down gingerly, but he won't let go. He hangs on to her arm, leads her over to the swing.

"Push me," he says. She helps him up, pulls him back, and lets go.

"So, Bob, how is married life treating you?" she says to her former fiancé. Though Kathy is still her best friend, she's rarely seen him since they broke up many moons ago.

"I love it," he says, concentrating on the intricacies of pushing Addie in the swing without upsetting the rhythm of the motion.

"What have you and Kathy been up to lately?"

"Not much. Taking care of the kids. I took them out to the Air and Space Museum's annex at Dulles to show them the Enola Gay," he says. "And, hey, I almost finished my book."

"Great," says Dee. "Our memorial was approved by Congress, though it's not on the Mall. It's in a park near the Capitol. The President is going to speak at the ribbon cutting."

"That's fantastic," gushes Bob.

Julian jumps off the swing and runs after Larry Spicer.

"I'm tired," whines Addie.

Kathy comes up. Helps her daughter off the swing. "How you doing, Dee?"

"Fine." They hug. Over Kathy's shoulder she sees Mitch talking to a skinny, hatchet-faced woman. A blond.

"Who's that?" she asks Kathy, pointing at the woman.

"Oh, Clara Dente. She and her husband are new to the club."

"I think I'll talk to her," says Dee.

She strolls over, wraps one arm around Mitch's waist, reaches out, and shakes Clara's hand.

"Hi, I'm Dee Wynn."

"Oh, your wife, Mitch?" asks Clara.

"No. No," he says. "Dee's an old friend. We were in college together."

"I haven't seen you around. You must be new to the club," says Dee.

"Yes, we recently moved from Seattle. Drake found a job with the Wildlife Federation. I work part time for a homeless shelter in downtown D.C. But mostly I raise kids."

"That's great," says Dee. She notices there are three other blonds at the party, one of whom she knows from Blair. No way Mitch would have anything to do with this do-gooder.

She draws Mitch aside. "Why haven't you called me?" She hates to show weakness, but she can't help it.

"I'm sorry. I've been busy."

"I thought after the night we spent together you really cared for me."

"I do, honestly, care for you," says Mitch, but she can tell he is lying, the way he looks around rather than at her. Barry Spicer bangs two metal plates together. Robin wants everyone to gather around the table for the Stork Club's fifth-anniversary cake cutting.

Dee never gets a chance to resume her conversation with Mitch nor to interview the other three blonds, but now she knows exactly what she's going to do. She heads back to her mom's house. Spends the rest of the day helping her clean up.

"You're such a sweetheart, Dee, to hang around with the old lady. You've always been the greatest sport. Helped raise your brothers and sisters." Dee can see her mother's on the verge of tears. "And I'm so glad that you started to think about marriage. But a divorced man, are you sure?"

"I'm thirty-nine. How many men do you think are available?"

"Yes, that's true. In my day, if you were thirty-nine, you were an old maid. But not today, and anyway, I don't think that would apply to you. You are a beautiful woman. The men would flock to you like bees to honey." She laughs, twists her hair around her finger. "Though I wonder why they haven't flocked to you before."

"I wasn't available, Mom."

"Yes, yes, that's it."

When it turns dark outside, Dee wanders upstairs to her room, rummages through her closet. Finds an old pair of jeans and a dark shirt. She tries them on. They're loose. Dee's pleased with herself. How many women pushing forty are thinner than they were in high school?

She heads downstairs. "Mom, can I borrow your car?" she asks. "I'm going over to visit a friend."

"In those old clothes?"

"We're going to play outside."

"You can't fool me. You're up to something," Dr. Wynn says, shaking her finger at her daughter. "I don't want to hear what it is, but sure, take the car."

Dee walks down the front steps. Opens the door. Climbs in the Subaru and starts the engine. She does not know who that woman was that Bull saw kissing Mitch at his front door, but she will find out.

Only once in her life has she resorted to these tactics. That was in Chicago, over Mitsy Mossi, a colleague of hers who always got the choice assignments. Dee hated this woman from the moment she set eyes on her. Mitsy dressed in tight clothes and spoke in a syrupy Southern accent. She said, 'I declare' this, 'I declare' that, all day long like a Junior Leaguer, though—with her frosted hair and tight clothes that revealed every contour of her compact, itsy-bitsy body—she seemed more like a Dallas cheerleader. She was a graduate

of the University of Alabama, the Harvard of the South. She
praised anything in pants in that syrupy accent of hers, even
the delivery boys. Once Dee saw her praise a rabbit-eared
Fed Ex boy who showed her a drawing—she told him how
to improve it and gushed about how smart he was. Natural
intelligence. Rabbit ears blushed and fell all over himself on
the way out. That's why Dee hated Mitsy, because she knew
how to manipulate not only the Fed Ex types, but every man
in the office, even the intelligent ones, and the old codgers who
gave out the assignments.

Dee drives up Grant to Carroll, takes a right, and follows
the turnaround to 410. She feels an unbelievable glow
of determination inside her as she takes a right on New
Hampshire.

It was a very simple thing that she did, she thinks. Exactly
what she is planning now, which is to take charge of a situation
that's getting out of hand before it's too late. With Mitsy, all
Dee did was alter one of her drawings. It was for a municipal
building somewhere. When the clients reviewed the drawing,
they couldn't believe what a stupid mistake she'd made. The
firm lost the contract. On the very same day, Mitsy lost her job
and the codgers moved Dee into Mitsy's old office. Dee felt
cheap, but not so cheap she wouldn't do the whole thing all
over again. You've got to use what you've got, she believed, to
get what you want.

Dee passes by the turn-off to Mitch's house. Takes a right
at the light on Eastern and another on Oak Lane. She parks
down the street, on the lower part of a hill, where the car can't
be observed. She gets out and follows the long shadow of an
abandoned warehouse. Crosses the street. Enters the woods
behind his house. She leans on a tree for a few moments,
waiting for her eyes to adjust to the darkness. Plunges in. She
follows the line of trees to the back of Mitch's house, her heart
pounding. She pauses. Checks the house. A light is on in the
kitchen. She can see the refrigerator. But no one is in there. No
lights on the second floor. She follows the tree line farther to
the side of the house, where she sees another light but can't

see inside the window. She hunches down and scurries across the open space between the woods and the house. She presses herself against the side of the building like a shadow. She's afraid. She hasn't crept around like this since she was a kid. She slides up very slowly, making sure that she's not making any noise, and peers in the window.

A lace curtain covers the window so the view inside is distorted. At first, she sees a television. Tuned to the Lifetime network. Why would Mitch be watching the woman's channel? She wonders. The window is open slightly, and now she can hear a female voice. Dee shifts her line of sight to the left and sees the blond reclining on a couch in Mitch's arms. Her eyes are closed. Her heart-shaped lips are opened in a sigh. Mitch is kissing her neck and shoulder. He fumbles clumsily with the button of her blouse and reaches behind her to unsnap her bra. He puts his mouth on her breast. "Oh, Mitch, darling," she moans. She takes his hand and moves it down between her legs. She's wearing pink panties trimmed in lace, a slit down the crotch.

"Slut," growls Dee, in a voice audible enough for the woman to hear. She leans up on her elbow and stares at the window.

"What's the matter?" asks Mitch.

The lady shakes her head in disbelief, squinting—she must make out the pair of spiteful eyes staring at her, because she covers her mouth with the back of one hand and screams.

Dee ducks. Scuttles back across the open space into the woods and dives behind a bush. She lies still. A screen door slams. Mitch slinks around the corner of the house, turning his head left and right slowly, scanning the woods for any sign of movement. He stops at the window and looks down at the ground. Scratches his head. Turns. Walks slowly over to the edge of the woods. Peers in. Dee's heart is in her throat. He follows the perimeter of the woods around to the back of the house until Dee can no longer see him. Then he walks back and stands only a few feet from the bush where she's hiding. Mitch shrugs and wheels around to leave when the bitch parts the curtain and lifts the window sash.

"Did you see anything out there?" she asks in a tremulous voice.

"No, nothing," he says in a soothing voice that makes Dee mad. He's coddling the bitch. "You must've imagined it. It could've been a reflection from the lights in the hallway."

"Those were eyes I swear, horrible yellow eyes like a wolf."

"A werewolf," he laughs.

"It's not funny," the woman says, shaking a finger at him and smiling as if it is. She closes the window and locks it. He walks around the house, looking back several times, as if he's afraid that he will be jumped from behind. Dee hears the front door click and then dead silence. The lights go off downstairs, leaving only the blue reflection of the TV screen against the lace curtains. Then the lights come on upstairs.

She lies as still as a frightened rabbit for five minutes, afraid that this might be a ruse. That they might be waiting by the window for her to move, and when she does, they'll chase after her like a pack of hounds. But this fear is only temporary, replaced by a fury that builds up inside her. She wants to seek revenge—nice, physical revenge—but she knows better. She is not a werewolf, as the blond imagines. She is a sensible woman with a superior brain and she will come up with a foolproof plan that will get her exactly what she wants, just like she did with Mitsy.

She gets to her feet slowly. Retraces her steps until she's at the other side of the house. Looks up at the light shining through the second-floor window. A wind comes up. The branch of a tree scraps the metal siding on the house. She bows her head and trudges for her mom's Subaru. She backs the car into a driveway and turns left toward Eastern Avenue, her hands shaking on the steering wheel.

Chapter Eight

It is the day after the picnic at Opal Daniels Park. Mitch Lovett and Gail Strickland are relaxing in a Jacuzzi, sipping champagne at the Antietam Inn, where Mitch stayed when he was hired by the National Park Service to film the memorial illumination for the 130th anniversary of the Civil War battle. Gail told him that Davy's Cub Scout pack had planned a camping trip and wouldn't return until late tomorrow evening and, with Ed in Salt Lake City, it was the perfect opportunity to steal some time together. Plus, it is isolated. Little chance of meeting friends from back home.

On a table next to the Jacuzzi is a bowl full of chocolate-covered strawberries. Gail plucks one from the bowl and nibbles it while Mitch nibbles her neck and shoulders. He dives under the water to nibble her breasts. The bubbles from the jets titillate his crotch, and he stifles a desire to take her right this moment in the tub, because something has been bothering him all during the drive up from Takoma Park.

"I wish you had asked Ed for a divorce," confesses Mitch, as he surfaces and sips the champagne. "But I understand why you didn't. No telling how he would react."

"He'd murder me," says Gail, leaning closer to Mitch as if for protection. "Why don't we run off to the other side of the world, instead. Australia. New Zealand. No one would ever find us again."

"That wouldn't be fair to my children," says Mitch, brushing shoulders with her. "I mean, I would love to run off with you, but it isn't the right thing to do. We have to face reality. Somehow we'll manage the divorce problem, and then, we'll move in together, maybe around here. I have contacts in Frederick. We'll buy a house. I'll find a job, and we'll live happily ever after. That is, if I'm not presuming too much."

"You're not," says Gail, as she pours another glass of champagne for both of them. "Not as far as I am concerned. But I don't think Ed would approve of any plans we might make. I think the only way he would approve is if somehow we eliminate the son of a bitch. Maybe we can throw him off a cliff—though that might be difficult since he's probably stronger than both of us put together."

"We could drug him first."

"Yes, that could be arranged. I will have a little get-together with Ed like I am with you now. I'll lace Ed's champagne with, let's see, the date-rape drug. He'll be so compliant he'll throw himself off the cliff."

"That sounds like a reasonable solution," says Mitch Lovett, chucking her under the chin lovingly. "But I don't think I want to do that."

"Nor do I, really." She starts crying. Mitch holds her. "It's just that I feel so trapped. I don't know what to do."

Later, after they dry off, they jump into bed and make love, but it is a tired, dull love that reminds him of his last moments with Kathy. Like their minds are on something else and they are simply going through the motions.

"You know, darling," says Mitch, as they lay on their backs staring at the ceiling fan going around and around, "I think I'm more in love with you now than ever, but we need to do something about Ed before it kills our relationship."

"There's nothing we can do," says Gail. She takes his hand and squeezes it. "Ed is a baby. If you hurt his feelings, there's no telling what he will do—but I almost guarantee, it will be violent."

In the morning, they tour the battlefield. It is raining lightly, and they had thought to bring their raincoats. They are in shorts and hiking boots, and they purchase caps at the visitors' center along with a guidebook. They stop at the West Woods, and at the Cornfield, where Union troops were slaughtered charging the Confederate lines. They see a sign noting that General Hooker led the charge in this part of the battlefield. Gail tells Mitch that hookers were named after the general, who was known for visiting the brothels in Washington when off-duty.

"You're full of interesting information," he laughs.

On the way in, they noticed another couple, a man with his arm around a woman so tightly he seemed to crush her. They could see the painful expression on the woman's face— or maybe it wasn't pain. Maybe it was desire. It was hard to tell. They see this couple at other stops, at Dunker Church and Bloody Angle. He still clasps her tightly, and the look on her face is unaltered except it seems now a bit more on the blank side. He holds an umbrella over their head. It has started raining harder. Gail tells Mitch she bets anything that the man is an abuser.

"You see the look on his face. Determined, like he isn't ever going to let her go."

Mitch hadn't noticed the look, but he did at the next stop, exactly as Gail said. Determined. "But that could mean anything. Maybe he's determined to keep the lady dry."

"Did you see her expression? She's afraid."

"Maybe she doesn't like water."

He puts his arm around Gail as they head back to the parking lot. They move the car to the lot on the bluffs above Burnside's Bridge and hike down a winding path until they come to a bench. Mitch wipes the seat with a towel he found in the car. They sit down and stare at the bridge, which is made out of limestone from a local quarry, according to the guide that Mitch reads out loud. It has been there since 1830. Built by the Dunkers. Muddy Antietam Creek flows beneath the bridge. "It must've flowed with blood in 1862," says Gail, sighing. "I can almost hear the soldiers screaming."

"Those aren't soldiers," says Mitch as he turns to look up the path. The couple they saw earlier appear from around a depression in the hill. They are arguing. The umbrella sways from side to side as the man pokes his finger in the woman's face to make a point. Then he notices Mitch and Gail sitting on the bench staring at him wide-eyed. "Candice fell," he says, smiling weakly.

"Yes, I fell. The ground is wet," she says, looking at the man as if she is seeking approval. He smiles at her, touches her cheek gently where there seems to be a bruise.

"You hurt yourself."

"Yes, I hit something hard when I fell." Mitch and Gail surrender their seats. The injured lady sits down heavily on the bench. "I ruined my pedal pushers," Candice sniffs.

Mitch looks down at the torn, grass-stained knee of her pink pants and wonders how she could both land on her knee and bruise her cheek at the same time when she fell. He looks over at Gail, who must've been wondering as well. She nods toward the man as if she wants Mitch to say something. But he doesn't.

"I feel a touch dizzy," says Candice. She is a tall, lithe brunet with a weathered face and too much red lipstick.

"Maybe you have a concussion," says Gail in a concerned voice. "Maybe a doctor should check you out."

"No, no, no," says the man too quickly. "She'll be all right. It's only her low blood pressure."

"Earl is right," the woman says, waving off Gail's concern. She has a twang in her voice. "I get these dizzy spells all the time. Just let me sit here for a while. I'll be fine."

Earl smiles down at her, and she smiles back wanly. He hands her the umbrella to keep her dry. Earl wears a yellow rain slicker. He pulls the hood over his head and clasps his hands together. "Burnside's Bridge. Can you believe these fool Yankees couldn't come up with a better way of getting at General Toombs's four hundred Georgians up there on that hill in rifle-pits than to charge across that old limestone bridge five abreast? The bodies piled up so high that those boys rushing from behind used them as stepping stones to storm the bluffs."

On the way back to the parking lot, Gail tells Mitch that she has seen enough. She is too wet and tired and disgusted to go on. "Why didn't you say something to that man, Earl?"

"Because I wasn't sure anything was happening," he answers, opening the door of the Saab for her. "You need to take people at their word. And that lady, Candice, backed up Earl, so what was I to do?"

Mitch jumps in his side of the car, turns on the defrost and heat so they can dry off.

"Perhaps you're right," Gail says. "You never know what happens behind closed doors. But my intuition tells me that whatever it is, it isn't pretty."

"My intuition tells me the same. It also tells me to mind my own business." He pulls out of the lot and follows the winding road to Sharpsburg. They decide to parallel the river to Harpers Ferry before they turn northeast at Point of Rocks, skirting the congestion of Frederick. The wipers slap against the windshield. Mitch turns off the heat and turns on the radio to a rock station.

"It's stuffy in here."

He turns on the AC.

For the most part, they are silent as they check out the scenery outside their rain-streaked windows. They wind up and down the hills, past cow pastures where the cows gather under trees, their backsides to the wind that is coming off the river. Only a few are sitting down, as cows are supposed to in the rain. They pass groves of trees and fields planted mostly in corn that is near to chest high. They slow for a small town lined with clapboard houses and small front yards, some neglected and falling apart, but most in good shape, flowers and vegetable gardens in the yard. They pass through the block-long business district, boutique stores, a bar, a small market, a few churches, and then drive out into the country.

"I don't know what I would do if I lived out here," says Gail. Mitch feels like there is a sense of doom hanging over them now. He doesn't know whether it has to do with his relationship with Gail or Gail's relationship with Ed. But whatever it is, he is afraid.

When they turn north, the rain turns to drizzle. They approach another small town. The rain stops. They pass an antique mall housed in a red barn, and Gail asks Mitch to turn around. He does. He pulls into a parking lot, and as he is about to climb out of the car, Gail grabs his arm. "I want to talk."

He falls back in his seat. Switches on the ignition. The AC blows at them full blast. He turns it down a nudge. "Okay, what's on your mind?" He turns toward her and, for a moment, is caught by her beauty. Her skin is unblemished except for a tiny patch of freckles across her nose—he loves subtle imperfections. They define the beauty. Her light-blue eyes are the color of what? The patch of blue that appears from behind the clouds after a rainstorm. Her blond hair. He blushes at the thought, but he can't help it. He doesn't want to lose Gail.

She looks at him with the same intensity, and then they break off.

"I have been thinking all the way down here, what if my intuition is correct? What if Earl is an abuser? What would I do if I were Candice, after many long years of abuse? It becomes a pattern, you know, like smoking. The longer you do it, the harder it is to quit. What if Candice had a grown-up son who is in an abusive relationship now, just like his parents? That's another pattern. Like father, like son."

"Tell me about it," says Mitch, relieved that it is her relationship with Ed that is concerning her.

"I don't want to be like that," she says with fervor. "I mean, it's one thing for me to be abused. I'm a grown-up. I can handle it. Well, maybe I can—it's been going on way too long already. But to visit it upon Davy—I can't let that happen. I'm his mother, after all. You understand what I mean."

"Yes, perfectly," says Mitch, shaking his head, "at least I understand in a way. I never had a mother."

"I know you didn't." She leans over and kisses him on the cheek, not the reaction he wants. He doesn't want her to feel sorry for him.

"But Davy has a mother, and I don't plan to let him down," she says, leaning back in her seat with a sigh. "Like Candice maybe let her son down. I don't want to be like that lady—though of course I'm just imagining this. I don't know if she has a son. But I know she's scared, and, when I look at her, I see myself years from now unless I stand up for myself and Davy, no matter what the consequences. So what I'm getting at is that I plan to tell Ed that I want a divorce. I mean it this time."

They wander down the aisles in the antique mall and then halt to browse at a stall of faded highway maps. Mitch opens an Esso map of Virginia from the thirties. He follows the red line of a road that no longer exists as it winds up the Blue Ridge Mountains to a town that also probably no longer exists, because it's inside the park boundary near Old Rag Mountain. Gail looks over his shoulder.

"Hey, that's where Ed and I camped a week ago," she says, snickering in a lighthearted way, as if everything has already been settled. "Won't camp out with that creep ever again as long as I live."

Mitch checks out a set of leather postcards, some addressed to Ollie Greene in New York at an APO address. "Doesn't that mean that Ollie was in the army?"

"I think so. The A stands for army. It's a distribution address." She checks the postmark. "It's dated 1918. World War One." She rifles through the postcards until she comes to one addressed to a woman, Helen Steward, from the same Ollie Greene. "Love letters, I bet."

"Oh, they're not love letters," says Mitch kiddingly. "Why write a love letter on a postcard where everybody can see?"

"Maybe because you want the whole world to know." She squeezes his arm.

"Unlike us."

"Yeah," she laughs.

They browse through a collection of commemorative plates and spoons, mostly of world fairs but one set of presidents, another of generals; old clocks and watches, three cuckoos on the wall that go off at once; a Barbie doll collection, a bin of Barbie and Ken body parts, and another of Victorian dolls, some decapitated; old magazines, including *Look, Saturday Evening Post*, and one *Collier's* so brittle a page falls apart in Mitch's hand; a collection of Civil War mementos, mostly framed minié balls, a few rusty swords and sidearms; and, in the front of the store, a collection of furniture, including a corner cupboard, a dinged-up rolltop desk, and a dining room table that sits eight, with chairs to match. "You know, Gail," says Mitch, pointing across the street at a big brick house with a wraparound porch, "why don't we buy that house and furnish it with all this stuff?" He waves his hand at the depressing collection of antiques in the mall.

"I imagine that's all we could afford after purchasing the house."

"You'd be surprised how inexpensive real estate is out here," says Mitch.

They wander out to the car and climb in. Take one last look at the big brick house with green awnings and a collection of evergreens in the yard.

"It's only eight miles from Frederick, an ideal place for us to live if we wanted to."

"Yes, very ideal," says Gail, thoughtfully as they pull out onto the road. "I think you're right. I think that I'm madly in love with you and it would be wonderful to live with you here for the rest of our lives. I could work in the antique store. Lord knows they probably need help. You could find a job in Frederick through your contacts. Davy would be happy here, and so would your kids when they come to visit. Or maybe I am assuming too much?"

"You're not."

"Well, then, first things first."

Mitch pulls onto Route 28 toward Rockville and the interstate. He sees a reflection of Gail's determined face in the windshield as it drifts along with the landscape and feels a sudden chill at the back of his neck. He wonders if Gail is taking on more than she can handle.

Chapter Nine

Gail Strickland chops lettuce for the salad. Slices the tomatoes in small pieces the way her son prefers. She runs outside to flip the hamburgers on the grill. She breaks open a bag of Tater Tots and heats them in the oven. She's going through the motions, but her heart isn't in it. The resolve she felt the day she came back from the Antietam Inn is still there, it's just that she hasn't found the opportunity to tell Ed that she wants a divorce because, apparently, he's decided to turn over a new leaf.

"I know I haven't been a very good husband, but I'll tell you what," he said his first night home from the conference, after they put Davy to bed. "They had this session in Salt Lake about coaches who were former athletes. How they may have never dealt with what it was like to be out of the limelight. We're in shock. Like our life ended when we quit sports and now we have to create a new one.

"I never did that," he said sadly, patting her hand.

As a way of proving his resolve, Ed took Gail out to a play at the Round House Theatre, a romantic comedy. Then he took her out to dinner at The Melting Pot. A few nights later, he took her dancing at Surf Club Live. He was on the floor all night, hugging her closely for the slow dances, and twirling her around for the fast ones until she was exhausted. She went through the motions that night in bed, and she knew that Ed was disappointed at her lack of response, but he didn't say a word. On the domestic scene, he took out the trash, washed the dishes, vacuumed the rugs, shopped for groceries once— he even bought her a pair of earrings she had admired at Now and Then. He took Davy for long walks when Gail was tired. Tossed a football with him. Helped him build a fort in a tree in the backyard, though it fell down in a windstorm the night they finished.

The oven timer goes off. She checks the Tater Tots. They're ready, and she turns down the heat so they stay warm. Takes the salad to the dining room table with two bottles of dressing, balsamic vinaigrette for herself, ranch for the boys. Then she rushes out to retrieve the hamburgers from the grill, thinking about how she is caught between a rock and a hard place. She has felt this numerous times in her marriage and, as before, has not a clue what to do.

She hears a branch cracking underfoot behind her. She whips around. It is Ed, home early from his first day of summer practice.

"Oh, you scared me," she says.

He leans against the gate casually and stares at her, a stare that goes straight through her, as though she's invisible. In his hand, he's holding a pink envelope.

"Look at this," he says, handing the envelope to her. "I found it in my desk drawer when I was looking for a pencil after practice."

Gail opens the envelope. Unfolds the paper. It looks like a ransom note, with letters cut from a newspaper and pasted to the paper. She reads,

To Ed Strickland

While you were in Salt Lake City your wife was FUCKING Mitch Lovett every day for a week. Thought you ought to know.

A Friend

Gail drops the envelope on the ground. Looks up at Ed.

"Is it true?" he asks her. This time his eyes are focused straight on hers, as if by looking in her eyes he can tell the truth no matter what she says.

"No, it's a lie. Somebody, I don't know who, a-a devious, conniving person," she sputters, "is trying to get between you and me and hurt Mitch in the bargain."

He leans down. Picks up the paper. Turns it over. "This devious person, whoever he is, took all the letters from the *Washington Post*. I mean look at the *W-h* in the first sentence and the *t-o* in *To*—it comes from the masthead. Then look at all the capital letters in *FUCKING*. Headlines. Can you believe all the trouble this devious person went to?

"In addition to that," he says, moving closer to Gail—she's backed up to the grill, "this devious person went through a hell of a lot of trouble to deliver the letter to my office and put it in my drawer. I asked the janitor. He didn't see anyone in my office. So whoever this was knows his way around Blair. A graduate. Rex Milsap. Barry Spicer. Bull. Bull had a crush on you in high school. Maybe he still does."

"That's the craziest thing I ever heard. He's in love with Paula Wells."

"Maybe yes, maybe no. You don't see him marrying her," says Ed, shaking his finger in his wife's face. "I can see this as the perfect opportunity for Bull. Kill two birds with one stone."

"Oh, please, Bull hasn't done anything. I swear to God," she says, stepping sideways. The edge of the grill is burning her butt. She turns around. Scoops the hamburgers onto a plate. She heads into the kitchen. Turns off the oven. Tosses the Tater Tots in a bowl, gathers up the condiments, and takes them all to the dining room table, where she lines them up neatly around the salad.

Ed is standing inside the kitchen door, arms folded across his chest, watching her. Gail feels a sense of dread, like she's in the eye of a hurricane, has been for the past three weeks, and now the winds are picking up.

She hurries into Davy's bedroom. He's still napping. A bunch of soldiers he was playing with before he fell asleep are scattered on the pillow. She closes the door. Heads back to the kitchen. Ed is still standing at the same spot.

"Okay, maybe you're right. Maybe Bull doesn't have anything to do with this. But that doesn't change what's in the letter," he says in a controlled voice. "I mean, whoever wrote this letter says you have been fucking Mitch Lovett. Is it true? Have you been fucking Mitch Lovett?"

"I haven't, I swear to God, I haven't slept with anyone other than you."

"Fucking. Fucking is the word."

"Please, Ed. Davy's in the next room."

"He's asleep."

"Okay, fucking."

"I don't believe you." Ed walks up to the kitchen table. Grabs a chair and throws it against a wall. "You're telling me a goddamn lie."

Gail backs up into the dining room. Ed follows. "You want to know something?" he asks. "I don't think you ever loved me. Maybe for a moment after we got married, but that's it. I don't even think you wanted a baby."

"That's not true. I wanted a baby."

"But you didn't want me."

"I didn't say that," she asserts. "We've had our problems, but we could have worked things out if you were willing to put some time into it. We could've had a better relationship."

"Oh, that's all bullshit. That's what a marriage counselor would say." He pulls out one of the dining room chairs. Sits down. Covers his face and talks through his hands. "The real truth is that you don't give a damn."

"Who are you to talk about giving a damn?" asks Gail, moving away from the table. Turning toward him. "When you admitted a couple weeks ago you were not a very good husband, you were right. You spend too much time at work or hunting or smoking dope with your buddies or whatever you're up to. And you treat us like crap. Whack Davy in the head when you feel like it. Scream at me. Call me names. Tell me I'm a dominating bitch."

"That's not happening anymore. I've reformed," he says, peeking between his fingers, as if surprised by her stance.

"Besides, what if I neglected you and Davy somewhat? That's not half as bad as what you've done. I never slept with another woman."

"I wish you would." Now she is upset, even though many people would think she doesn't have a leg to stand on. "You don't care for me or Davy. Find another woman. Make yourself happy. We do not belong together."

He shakes his head, looks down at the ground. "Yes, we do. We had a fine time together the other weekend in White Oak Canyon. We made love. You said you enjoyed it."

"There's more to a relationship than making love. Besides…" She hesitates, thinking that it might not be a good idea to insult his masculinity.

"Besides what?"

"Besides, I don't know, you need someone who can fulfill all your needs, not just the physical kind."

"Are you saying I'm some kind of freak? That you have to coddle me like a baby or something?"

"I'm not saying that. I'm saying that we're not compatible. We need to get a divorce and get on with our lives."

He drops his hands and looks up at her, narrowing his eyes. "You're such a fucking bitch," he growls, "trying to blame me, as if it was my fault you screwed that scum bag."

She denies once again that she screwed Mitch, but Ed is beyond believing her lies. He stands up. Throws the chair aside. It bangs against the buffet that used to be in her parents' dining room. Makes a nasty gash in the wood. She flees to the living room. Positions herself between Ed and the door to Davy's room. He pursues her but stops at the mantelpiece to grab the battered Civil War era tin cup and fling it across the room. The flowers in it scatter in every direction. "You love your antiques more than you love me," he snarls. She makes a move to retrieve the cup, but he flings her around and slaps her hard in the face, hard enough to snap her head back.

"How dare you," she cries back. She touches her cheek where it stings and throws herself at him. But he steps aside, grabs her by the hair, slaps her two more times so hard it rattles her brain, and flings her on the couch like he's discarding a rag doll. He's breathing hard. Looks around the floor. Sees Davy's Power Ranger tennis shoes and a Power Ranger action figure. Socks. Underwear. Belt. He grabs the belt and raises his hand. Gail knows that it would be useless to resist any further and turns away to receive the blows on her back. But they don't come. She peeks over her shoulder.

Davy is standing at the door of his room, his hand on the doorknob, staring wide-eyed at his father. "What's going on?" he asks in a tiny voice.

Ed throws the belt on the floor. Meets his son's gaze.

"Don't you dare go near him," says Gail. She rises from the sofa. Ed looks at her as if he's in a dream. Backs off. Leaves the room. She hears the back door slam. She's afraid of what's going to happen next—afraid that he's going out to the shed, where he keeps his guns locked up. But then she sees him marching around the side of the house. He jumps in his black Nissan pickup and takes one more menacing look at the house. Then he guns the engine and screeches down the street, leaving a trail of rubber behind him.

Chapter Ten

G et dressed, honey," says Gail, watching the taillights of the truck as it disappears around a corner up the street. "We're leaving."

"Did Daddy hurt you?" her son asks in the same tiny voice. He touches her cheek where Ed slapped her. She winces.

"It's not bad," she says, smiling bravely. It's a war wound, she thinks. *What a small price to pay to get rid of the bastard.* "Get dressed now."

Davy grabs his Power Ranger shoes and heads back to his room. Gail packs for both of them, and they rush out the back, where she picks up the pink envelope and offending letter still lying on the ground. *They might be important*, she thinks. *Evidence.* She heads around the corner of the house, checks up and down the street to make sure he hasn't returned. She is afraid she will lose her nerve. A neighbor from across the street waves at her. She waves back.

"What's going on, Mom?" asks Davy, trailing behind her so slowly that she has to drag him. "Where are we going?"

"We'll go to Robin's house," she says. They cross Carroll Avenue near Savory. A few of her friends are sitting under the umbrella sipping tea. It is early evening. They have just come home from work. They wave at Gail as she passes by on the sidewalk and watch her head down to Columbia with a bruise on her cheek and big grin on her face as if she won the lottery. Gail doesn't know what they must be thinking nor does she really care at this point. She takes a right on Hickory Street and suddenly panics. What if Robin isn't home? She picks up her pace until she sees the house clearly. Robin is on the back deck watching her kids play in the yard. Gail walks around the side of the house.

"Hi, Robin," she yells up at her.

Robin turns around. "Gail." She smiles. "Come up."

Davy tugs at her hand and points at his friends.

"You go play with Larry and Ruth." Davy hands her his bag and runs down the hill. Gail climbs the stairs to the deck. Sits down in a chair. Robin looks at their bags, a puzzled expression on her face.

"Would you like something to drink?" she asks, finally. "Iced tea? Coffee?"

"Sure. Whatever's easiest to fix."

Robin disappears inside the house. Comes out a few moments later with two glasses of iced tea. Hands one to Gail. Sits down. "I like to hang out here in the evening when I get a chance. Watch the kids play and the birds singing in the trees and the sun moving toward the horizon," she says, sighing. "It's so pleasant. What's with the bags?"

Gail sits on the edge of the chair, thinking about how she's going to explain herself. "I'm leaving Ed. I need a place for Davy and me to stay temporarily."

"Well, then, I insist that you stay here," says Robin. She puts down her glass. Stands up. Leans down and hugs Gail. Gail cries crocodile tears onto her shoulder. Dries her eyes with the paper towel Robin hands her.

"Thank you, Robin," she says. "You're a great friend. The best."

"You can tell me about it if you want to," says Robin, resuming her chair. She looks out at the kids. Larry and Davy are launching acorns in the air. Trying to catch them, one, two, three at a time. Ruth sits on a rock staring at them. Bored.

"Mom," she yells. "I'm going next door. I want to play with girls."

"Okay." Robin waves at her. Turns back to Gail. "He hit you. I can see a bruise on your cheek."

"Oh, I need to cover that up." She touches her cheek. "Yes, he hit me, but he could've done worse." She tells her about the belt and Davy standing in the doorway.

"That's horrible when a kid's involved."

"I know. That's one of the main reasons I'm leaving. The other is that I'm fed up with taking abuse from him, on and off, year after year."

"We all have our limits," says Robin, shaking her head sadly. "You know, I don't think I could ever, ever take that kind of abuse from Barry. It would crush my soul."

"It's not as simple as that," says Gail. She gazes intently at her friend. She has known her forever. They have traded secrets since childhood. Robin has never betrayed her. "I want to tell you something, but you must promise not to tell anyone else."

"Not even Barry?" She smiles weakly as if this will be a difficult task.

"Not even Barry, or any of our friends. It could be dangerous if it got around."

"I promise." Robin crosses her heart, as they always do when they reveal secrets.

"Remember a couple of months ago when we had a girls' night out at Republic and Dee came in?"

"Yes," says Robin. She seems to hold her breathe in anticipation.

"Remember that you told us that Bull told Barry that he saw Mitch kissing Dee in front of Mitch's house on Oak Lane?" Gail asks hesitantly. "That wasn't Dee. That was me."

"I knew it," says Robin. "I knew you always had a crush on Mitch, ever since college. I knew the first time you met him at that beer blast at Maryland, the way you looked at each other, there'd be trouble down the road."

"How could you know that?"

"I guess it was something I filed away in the back of my mind. And now that you say it out loud, I'm not the least surprised."

"You're right. I always had a soft spot for Mitch. But he was in love with Kathy, and I was married to Ed. There was nothing I could do until..."

"Until Mitch got divorced."

"Exactly," says Gail, sighing. "And that's the problem. This whole situation is my fault. A couple of months ago Dee told me that she had been sleeping with Mitch. I don't know why she did that?"

"She was staking out her claim."

"That's the way Kathy felt." Gail groans. "So first I'm jealous, second I have a fight with Ed, and third I rush over as fast as I can to Mitch's house. I'm such a coward. I should have done what I'm doing now instead of involving another person. Then there's this."

She hands Robin the pink envelope. Robin opens it and reads the contents. She shakes her head. "My first inclination is to say Dee wrote this, but she can't be that stupid."

"Who knows, when it comes to love?"

"That's true, but you know…" says Robin, trying to pull all this information together. "You know, you're trying to blame yourself for this, but I'm not sure that's it. Mitch invited you in. Then there's the fact that Ed abused you all these years, and that he's a scary guy. I mean, where could you turn? You could've moved to another state or entered a battered woman's shelter. But you know how things work out when you're dealing with a crazy man. Not even a restraining order stops them.

"Then there's this letter." Robin holds it in her hand and shakes it. "Writing this is like waving a red cape in front of a bull."

Gail spends the next few days worried to death about what to do next. She feels like a leaf that has fallen in the river, caught up in the current without any direction. Robin wants her to stay in Takoma Park at her house. They will protect her, though Gail can tell Barry is somewhat leery—he probably can't imagine defending his family against an irate Ed Strickland. Rex Milsap feels the same. Clara Dente knows a friend in Seattle who would take her and Davy in until things cool down. But that's too much to ask.

Mitch calls Gail several times, but she won't answer her cell. She's not sure why. In the last call he leaves a message that he's on a shoot in Austin, Texas, and will be back in three days, though he's anxious because he heard rumors that she broke up with Ed. He wants to see her when he returns, and

Gail agrees, but not for the reason Mitch desires. She is tired of drifting in the current.

Three days later Bull Carlton saunters up the walk to Robin's house to deliver a message from Ed: Gail needs to pick up the rest of her clothes or Ed will give them to Goodwill.

"I'm sorry," he says, looking down at his shoes, embarrassed, "that you and Ed are splitting up."

"Did he tell you why?"

"Nope, didn't say a darn thing." Bull looks at her expectantly, as if she is going to fill in the gaps.

But she just smiles. Thanks him.

He nods, hands her an envelope, and departs.

Gail rips open the envelope. Inside is a check for five hundred dollars and a note.

Dear Gail,

I will continue to take care of David because it is my responsibility. Also, it is my responsibility to make sure David grows up in a wholesome environment. Therefore, I am hiring a lawyer to win legal possession of my son with no visitation rights for you. I think everyone would agree that a whore should not raise a child.

Yours truly,
Ed Strickland

The first thing Gail thinks is that Ed should not call her a whore. She's an adulterer. She may lie. She may cheat. But she doesn't exchange sex for money. The second thing she thinks is that she might lose Davy. That would be the worst possible outcome. She doesn't trust the courts. Though they usually award custody to women, in this case, when she was the one who strayed, they might make an exception.

This letter only hardens her resolve about what she ought to do about her relationship with Mitch Lovett. She feels a sense of purpose that she hasn't felt in many years, almost like she's another person. She calls Mitch on the cell phone, and they agree to meet downtown for lunch at Childe Harold. She takes the Metro.

He's waiting at the bar when she comes in the restaurant. They find a table in a dark corner at the far end of the room away from the bar. Sit down. He orders a beer. She orders a glass of red wine. They hold hands across the table.

"I think I would like to drink one glass of wine after another until I'm drunk," she says, laughing nervously.

"I heard that you walked out on Ed," says Mitch.

"I'm sure it's all over town."

"Why?"

"It's not what you think." She shows him the note in the pink envelope.

"Damn, unbelievable," he says after having read it over several times and handing it back to her. "We were careful. How could anyone have found out?"

"You know the answer to that," she says, stuffing the note back in the envelope.

"Yeah, I probably do." Mitch groans. Withdraws his hands. Flags down the waiter. They order another drink.

"You know, Mitch, Dee wants you in the worst way. Maybe you should give her a chance."

"What do you mean by that?" asks Mitch. "I thought I made it clear to you that Dee is in the past. You're the one I want to be with."

"I know," she says. "That's the other reason I wanted to talk to you. Here." She reaches into her purse. Hands him the note that Bull handed her.

He reads it. Slams it down on the table. "That bastard. All he's trying to do is get even with you."

"That's right. He doesn't give a crap about Davy. But," she says, "there's more than a remote possibility that he could win custody of our son. He doesn't have a lot of money to spare, but he has powerful friends—boosters at Blair who look up to him because he was once the star of the football team when they were geeky water boys. One of them is a divorce lawyer. I'm sure he would handle Ed's case pro bono. So, you see, I don't stand much of a chance unless I can raise the money to hire a lawyer of my own."

"I'll help you out."

"No, I don't want your help. I inherited some money from my parents. I'm looking for a job downtown that pays benefits and enough money so that, with my inheritance, I can afford an apartment in a place like McLean Gardens. There's a nice elementary school nearby."

"Yeah, I'm truly glad that you seem to be landing on your feet," says Mitch, "but then how about us?"

"That's the thing, Mitch." She wants to get this over quickly. "I love you, but I love my son, too. I don't want to lose him. I mean, it's bad enough now, but if we kept up our relationship—you know."

"Yeah. Sure. I get what you're aiming at." She can tell that he's upset. His eyes are narrowing. But then he surprises her. "I know that Davy is as important to you as Addie and Julian are to me. I understand perfectly. We can break it off for a while, and after you win custody, we can get back together."

"I don't know, Mitch," she says, squeezing his hand. "I've been wandering from man to man since I left high school. I don't know if it's a good idea to get back together. I need some time to think things over."

"I can understand that as well. Sometimes I feel the same way myself." Though she can tell by the way he withdraws his hand and forces a smile, he doesn't mean it.

"But, you know, you need to forgive me. I'm still committed to our relationship. I mean, one day I'll feel better, but right now I'm thinking—what? I thought we worked things out at the Antietam Inn. I could understand your wanting to lay low for a while, but forever?"

The afternoon crowd trickles in. It gets noisier on the bar side of the dining room, which is mostly full of businessmen and women, conventioneers from the Hilton up the street out for a good time. Gail and Mitch stare at the crowd. Then they stare at each other.

"I didn't say forever. I need to think things over. Maybe we'll get together again. Maybe not," she says. "You know how it is with custody. The courts can change their minds."

"Yeah, they can," he says. He slaps his hand on the table. "Okay. I guess I have no choice. We'll play this thing by ear. Whatever happens, happens."

"I'm glad you see it that way," she says. She reaches out her hand. He pulls his hand away and stands up. He reaches in his pocket and pulls out some dollar bills. Places them on top of the check. Wheels around. Departs out of the front door. Walks up the street. She can see him pass by a window, head down and hands in his pocket.

She finishes her wine. Leaves an extra tip and exits through the door across 20th Street to the Metro.

Gail stares at herself in the window of the Metro as it pulls out of Dupont Circle Station. She is an attractive woman, with blond, wavy hair she keeps shoulder length and a thin, angular face. Hazel-colored eyes like Mitch's. Heart-shaped lips. When she turned thirty, nine years ago, she lost her baby fat, it seemed, overnight. Recently the lines began etching their way onto her face, but she imagines these add character and make her more desirable in a certain hardened, experienced way.

Not that she is experienced in any hard-nosed, worldly fashion. She's been drifting in the current for years, and now that she has decided to act, she is no longer afraid that it may end up in a mess as it did twenty-one years ago when she left for Denver University against her parent's wishes. She'll survive.

Chapter Eleven

Dee Wynn dresses carefully in a dark, ankle-length skirt. The waistline is tight to show off her figure. Her blouse is black, accenting her unblemished, pale skin, her prominent collarbone, and especially the V in the middle where her pulse beats, which she dabs with perfume. She rouges her high cheekbones slightly, outlines her eyes, and glosses her lips—she doesn't want to appear overly made up. She leans closer to the mirror. Perfect, she decides. She thinks she's contrasted the proper side of her—the soft skin, the long, swanlike neck, and the upturned nose—with the less proper, exotic side, her full lips and large, dark eyes.

On her way to the party, on the Metro, as she comes up out of the tunnel at Union Station to the rail yard—with its shacks, dilapidated Pullman cars, warehouses with broken windows, and walls of graffiti—she feels stupid. It doesn't help that two green-haired teenagers in leather jackets leer at her from a few seats away. *Why*, she thinks, *do I waste my time pursuing men? I have a job. I am a professional. That should be more than adequate.* But then there's this other side to her. Not that she falls for her mother's platitudes. It's just that you can only renovate so many public buildings, design so many postmodern structures, attend so many meetings and conferences, and have so many one-night stands until it becomes downright tiresome. She loves her job, but she wants to be loved back.

She worries about what she has done. It's not like with Mitsy Mossi. All she had to do was alter the drawings. No one could trace that back to her. Here it is easy to trace. Kathy, Robin, Barry, Bull, probably the whole membership of the Stork Club know, considering how fast news travels. Takoma Park may be at the edge of a big city, but it's a small town.

She wouldn't be surprised if they announced it in the *Takoma Voice*—that Mitch Lovett spent the night at her condo. That she was the blond that Bull saw on the lawn in front of Mitch's house. Or maybe they know that she isn't, depending on whether or not they read the note she put in Ed Strickland's desk. They might guess that it was she, the spurned lover, who put the note there. But then, anybody could've done it—Bull, Barry, Sonya—anyone who had it in for either Mitch or Gail. Even Ed could've faked it—or it could have been the effort of some do-gooder. There are plenty of do-gooders in Takoma Park, though more of the left leaning, not those on the right, who would be more shocked by adultery.

She exits the Metro at Takoma Park. Heads up the street, the sound of her heels clicking against the pavement. She crosses Laurel.

It is early October. The weather is mild. A balmy wind rustles the leaves in the treetops. The squirrels are scurrying around the park near the gazebo gathering acorns. The sun is close to the horizon. Turns the brown brick wall of the old folks home a golden color. Dee sighs.

There will be frigid days ahead, comfortable days, she hopes, when she and Mitch will warm themselves by a fire somewhere, a restaurant downtown—his abode, perhaps. Does he have a fireplace in that poor excuse of a home? She didn't see one when she peeked in the window. She'll have to convince him to sell the place. Combine their assets. Buy a new house in Adams Morgan or Mount Pleasant, maybe an imposing manse that overlooks Rock Creek Park. Or, better yet, they could move somewhere far away to a place that won't distract him. A place where they can focus on each other, one that appeals to Mitch because it will allow him to move his career in a more creative direction.

This is an act of will, she thinks as she heads down Carroll to Kathy's party. Everyone will be there from the Stork Club. No kids allowed, thank God. She wants to assert her power to control her emotions. She wants to live a reasonable life, but she seems to fail in her relationships. She discarded men like last year's fashionable outfit. Tom, Dick, Harry—she barely remembers their names though she can't help but remember the way things were with Bob Johnson.

She moved in to his townhouse in Georgetown, one of those with a bricked backyard, oriental rugs on the floor, and paintings of long-dead relatives on the wall. They had officially announced their engagement, but they were always at loggerheads—she figures it was because they were so much alike. They even fought about small things: the internal workings of cars when hers overheated; the kind of flowering plant that would grow best in the shade in his backyard; the best side of the bed for each of them to sleep on. He insisted the left, since he was left-handed.

One night they sat across from each other at the dinner table arguing about how to properly season chicken tagine, Bob pointing at the recipe in the Moroccan cookbook. Dee threw up her hands finally and told him that it was hopeless. "We are two people with logical, scientific minds who are in very similar fields. We always compete. We always have our guard up like we're always at work."

She marched upstairs, packed the two bags that she had brought with her from the condo, and called a cab. Bob followed her around the house professing his love, but she was adamant. When the cab came, he helped her take the bags out and made one more plea. It was a misty, foggy night. She turned and looked through the back window of the cab as it drove off. There he was, standing on the stoop in front of his house with his hands in his pockets and a look of agony on his face, and then he vanished in the fog like a character in a Bogart movie.

On this fall afternoon, Dee halts halfway down Woodland. The wind picks up, rocks the trees from side to side—they look like women with long hair bending low to listen to Dee's thoughts. She hears a whining noise. A helicopter clears a house then bends low, as if caught in the wind like the trees. It stalls for a moment. It seems about to crash but then picks up power and races toward Washington, its nose to the ground.

Dee shivers and remembers the agony on Bob Johnson's face as she left in the cab and of all the other ways she has treated men in a not to positive way. Men have done the same to her. She laughs. It's the war of the sexes. She wonders how Kathy managed to calm the beast in her former fiancée.

Dee wonders for a moment if she should call the whole thing off. Ditch Mitch Lovett. Confess to Ed and Gail. Move to another city. But, no, the wheels are already in motion. She couldn't stop it if she tried—besides she knows, deep down, she doesn't want to.

A dark cloud passes over and drops a smattering of rain. Dee races into Kathy's house and snakes her way through the crowd to the living room, where Bull Carlton is holding court by the fireplace. He is revealing to anyone who will listen that the other day, while hanging out with his best buddy, Gail Strickland sailed in in search of the clothes she'd left behind. Ed directed her to the bathroom, where she found them sopping wet in the bathtub.

"Her face turned red as a brick," says Bull, leaning against the mantelpiece casually, "and she grabbed the first thing she could find, a toilet brush. She attacked Ed with the brush, and he grabbed it from her and pretended to stick it in her mouth. 'You need to clean out your old toilet mouth,' he says, winking at me. 'No telling whose spuzz you been swallowing.' Then he ran off to his Nissan and raced up the street. Nearly hit a teenager. I haven't seen him since."

"That's truly pitiful," says Barry Spicer, sticking his hand in a bowl of potato chips on the mantel. "I almost feel sorry for the creep."

"He's not a creep. He's my buddy. I've known him since grade school and never seen him act this out of sorts. Well, sometimes with his father," reconsiders Bull, scratching his head, "or sometimes with other kids who got in his way."

"Seems to me he attacked you once when he thought you were paying too much attention to Gail," says Barry, munching on the chips.

"That's true. That's true," agrees Bull, shaking his head sadly. "But he was sorry afterward, and we were such close buddies—I mean, I ran interference for him on the football team at Blair and Maryland. So I forgave him even though he gave me a black eye. I'm still that way. I'm a loyal friend."

"What are you going to do?" asks Barry licking his fingers and sticking them back in the potato chip bowl. "Beat up Gail?"

"You keep eating those chips, you going to be as fat as a tick," says Bull, poking Barry in the side.

"Well, what are you going to do?" reiterates Barry.

"I'll tell you one thing I'm not going to do," Bull says, poking his friend again. "I'm not going to beat up a woman."

He looks straight at Dee who has been standing there the whole time faking a slow burn. "Why, don't you look hot, Dee," he says, grinning sheepishly and staring at her cleavage, "and smell good too."

"What's this all about?" she says, her voice cracking as if she's distressed. "Gail and Ed broke up because Gail was having an affair?"

"That's exactly it," says Bull, still staring at her cleavage, "with that old boyfriend of yours, Mitch Lovett."

Dee covers her mouth, faking shock. "Are you sure?"

"I'm sure," says Bull, nodding. Barry agrees.

"What proof do you have?"

"No proof. Just an educated guess."

"Then you're a couple of half-wits, spreading lies like that. You don't know Mitch like I do."

Bull pulls at his Fu Manchu. "I'm sure I don't know him like you," he says, grinning, "but that doesn't mean nothing other than, he's buggering both you and Gail."

"Oh, you're disgusting, Bull Carlton," she retorts, stamping her feet. She wheels around in faked outrage, makes her way through the kitchen, and steps out the back door, where a bar's set up. Robin Spicer hands her a margarita.

"Very tasty," she says as she licks the salt off the edge of the glass and swallows a large quantity of the green liquid.

Dee takes the margarita, sips it warily, and leans close to Robin. "What's this I hear about Gail and Ed breaking up because she was having an affair with Mitch Lovett?"

Robin tosses her head sadly. She finishes her drink and bangs the glass down on the table. "I thought you might have heard that through the grapevine."

"Yeah, I heard it, but I don't necessarily believe it."

"Well, I don't know if it happened or not. But if it did, I don't blame Gail. Ed Strickland is such a creep, and Mitch is no better, stringing both of you along."

Dee is about to launch into a defense of Mitch as she did with Bull. But then she leans against the deck railing. It groans less from her weight than from the shoddy condition of the wood. Kathy comes over and hugs her.

"Don't lean too hard on the railing," she says. She surveys the backyard—a swing set, a playhouse, and several plastic boxes overflowing with toys next to a line of trampled hostas. "I really ought to replace this deck, but I wanted to wait until the kids got older. They need a place to play that they can mess up."

"We're talking about Gail and Ed," says Robin. "You heard what happened at our house the other night."

Kathy grimaces. "I heard."

"What happened?" asks Dee.

"Ed drove up and down the street in that black pickup of his. He drove up on our lawn, fell out of the car onto the ground, and bellowed at the top of his lungs."

"Was he hurt?"

"No, he was drunk," says Kathy.

"He said that he wanted to see Gail. But Gail wasn't there."

"Where was she?"

"I don't know."

Dee hoped that Gail wasn't with Mitch. She knew that her plan wasn't foolproof even though she thought things out carefully. What she was counting on was Gail's instincts as a mother and Ed's short fuse. She can see that the fuse part is working.

Barry Spicer saunters up and grins disdainfully. "You girls gossiping again?"

"About what happened last night," says Robin.

"I was there. I went outside and told him to get his pickup off our lawn. He got up and kicked the tires a few times. He had an evil look in his eyes. He asked me if Davy was inside. I told him he was. Asleep. He said, 'Good. Let him sleep because in a few weeks he'll be sleeping in my house.' Then he climbed in the truck and raced off. He left a track a mile long on our lawn. I'm going to have to reseed it."

"You know what else?" says Robin. "He was over at Sonya's a couple of weeks ago and he said the very same thing. Gail was there. They got in a fight. Nearly beat each other up over it."

Kathy groans. "I don't have to listen to this," she mutters under her breath, excuses herself, and walks off.

Dee follows her. "Why don't you have to listen to this?" she asks.

"Oh, Dee, please."

"Come on, Kathy. I know you know something about your ex, and I can guess that it has to do with the rumors I've been hearing."

"What rumors?"

"That he's been sleeping with Gail."

Kathy looks at Dee sharply. "Okay," she says. "They're not rumors."

"You mean that Gail and Mitch…" Her voice cracks. She wonders if she comes off too anxious.

Kathy sighs, leans closer to her friend. "That's exactly what I mean."

"But how can you be sure?" asks Dee.

Kathy drags Dee off to a private corner of the yard by the trampled hostas where she can't be overheard. "This is something I want you to keep to yourself," Kathy says, squeezing Dee's shoulder. "Ed Strickland called me a while back. Drunk out of his skull and told me about an anonymous letter he found in the drawer of his office at Blair that said Mitch and Gail were sleeping together."

"That's incredible. How could you possibly believe a lie like that?" gasps Dee, trying to appear incredulous. "I mean, everybody might think that, but how can that be true? Mitch would never break up a marriage."

"Maybe not. Ed said that Gail denied it, though he didn't believe her. He threatened to hurt Mitch. Cave in his head with a baseball bat."

"That's horrible. Poor Mitch."

"Poor Mitch, nothing. I went over to that nasty house of his on Oak Lane the second I got off the phone and confronted him. It took about an hour for him to work up to an explanation, but finally he said, yes, he slept with Gail, but I didn't have to worry anymore because it was over."

"Oh, God, that's awful." Dee shakes her head sadly.

"Awful but true. I called Gail. She confirmed everything Mitch said."

"Oh, God." Dee covers her face. Starts to cry. Real tears. Her makeup is waterproof.

"That's not all. Gail told me she broke up with Mitch because she was afraid she'd lose custody of her kid otherwise. And she wants to swear off men for a while. Get some perspective, you know. Mitch is miserable. He loves her, he says." Kathy takes a deep breath. "I know this sounds kind of nutty, Dee," she continues, putting her arm around her friend's shoulder, "but Mitch's down in the basement right now. Getting bombed. Maybe you should try to calm him down."

"Yeah. Sure. Maybe he should try to calm me down." Dee can't believe her luck. "Maybe he should show me some respect."

"I know. I know," Kathy winces. "He's such a shit. He doesn't respect you. He doesn't respect the children or me. He didn't consider what people would think when he slept with Gail. I mean, I don't care about myself, but Addie and Julian, they're vulnerable."

"I know. Poor kids."

"I don't want to have to move out of town because of all the negative gossip. The kids making fun of Addie and Julian at school."

"I know. That's not what you want to do. Uproot your kids. Lose your friends," says Dee, pretending to think things over. "Okay, I don't know how it's going to help. The damage has already been done. But I'll go down there. I still like Mitch in spite of all this. I don't want him to do anything he would regret in the future. Like marry that bitch Gail"—she's having a hard time controlling her tone—"I'll make him forget she ever existed."

"That's the spirit, Dee." Kathy hugs her.

They wander back to the deck. Robin hands Kathy a margarita. Dee brushes by her friends and slips through the crowd to the basement door. She wanders down the stairs, trying to regain her composure. The TV is on to a sporting event of some sort. She can hear the cheering of a crowd, the drone of the announcer. She turns a corner at the bottom of the stairs. Mitch is sitting at the bar that Kathy installed after he moved out. She also installed a cabinet to house a big-screen TV, spray-painted the beamed ceiling white, and covered the cement floor with wall-to-wall carpeting.

Mitch waves at Dee. Smiles weakly. She can see the dimples at the corners of his thin, kissable lips. He is dressed in checkered black-and-white pants, a black long-sleeve shirt, and black shoes without socks. Reminds her of a chef at a trendy restaurant.

She walks in front of the TV. Looks at a baseball game. "The playoffs," says Mitch. "The score is one to one, I think, though I can't be sure." He waves his hand as if to dismiss the game.

"I didn't know you loved baseball."

"I do. I do." He squints at the screen. "Though I'm not sure which teams are playing."

"Certainly not Baltimore, or Bull and Barry would be down here." She climbs onto a stool next to Mitch and whispers in his ear that he is a real shit. "I mean, you must be really depressed sitting down here all alone while a party is going on upstairs. Maybe it's because everybody upstairs is talking about what you've been up to lately—screwing Gail Strickland."

"Oh, you've been talking to the wrong people," he laughs. Mixes a Tequila Sunrise. "The right ones think it's you I've been screwing. You want a drink?"

"Sure."

He hands her the one he's been fixing. Fixes another for himself. "But the right ones are wrong. I have been screwing Gail, but you don't have to worry about that anymore. She dumped me."

"Good."

"You're not upset?"

"About what, about your sleeping with Gail? Yeah, I'm upset. But you know what. I'm going to be entirely honest with you, Mitch. When I know what I want, I am going to get it. No one will stand in my way."

"Is that right?" says Mitch looking at her carefully. "You didn't, by any chance, put that note in Ed's desk at Blair did you?"

"What note? Oh, yeah. Kathy told me about it. No. That's like screwing your boss. I would never lower myself to that level. I'm straight up, above board. I can get what I want without resorting to subterfuge," she says looking at herself in the mirror behind the bar. Still looks good, but feels fairly bad. "I want you. I always have. From the moment I saw you, and Kathy stole you away. No one's going to steal you away again."

Mitch leans over, nibbles Dee's ear. Almost falls off his stool. Dee hefts him back up. "You're a sweetheart," he says, leaning his head on her shoulder.

"You're drunk. You need to go home and get some rest. You have your car here."

"No, I walked."

"Then I'll walk you home. I mean, you could get rolled. That's what happens to people who drink too much."

Chapter Twelve

Mitch Lovett feels fuzzy headed but not stupid. He knows what's on Dee's mind, and he can't say that he disagrees with her, only that he may be incapable of satisfying her. Not that it matters. He feels no obligation towards her, nor any desire other than the physical kind. Maybe he's a cad. But he doesn't care. It's hard enough to keep his footing.

"What's the hurry?" he asks. She's dragging him down Woodland toward his house. He's moving sideways, pushing her toward the curb.

"We've got to straighten you out, fellow, before you fade into oblivion." She pats him on the chest.

He stops. Weaves from side to side slightly.

"Are you okay?"

He grabs her arm. Turns her toward him. Kisses her on the mouth quickly. She moves back, leans against a telephone pole. They start kissing more intensely. Breathing hard.

A blue-haired old lady strolls down the street walking her dog. Looks at them, shaking her head. They break off. Head down Woodland. Dee snickers, "That was funny."

"Yes, it was," he says. He's not sure whether she's talking about the kissing or the blue-haired lady. He's very confused. They turn the corner toward Spring Park. He has to negotiate a bush that's overhanging a wall. He staggers into the street. A car swerves to miss him. He can see a fist shake at him from the driver's side window.

"Wow," he says, wiping his mouth. Dee helps him to his feet. "I think that sobered me up somewhat."

"I hope so. You could've gotten yourself killed," she says as they regain the sidewalk.

"Yeah, I could've ended up a hood ornament." He laughs. "I know what I need, a run in the park. That'll do the trick."

They're at the bottom of the hill. Mitch breaks off. Lurches across Poplar to the park. Pass the playground and up the hill to the soccer field. He runs around in circles. Dee shakes her head.

"What an idiot," she yells. She wanders up to Mitch, who's leaning on his knees. Breathing hard.

"You know what they do down south in bayou country?" he says, between gasps. "They get real drunk. Then they go out to a field and run around until they're sober. Then they get real drunk. Run around until they're sober."

"We're not going to do that," says Dee. "We're going to stay sober."

"Yeah, we'll stay sober."

They reach Oak Lane and wander across the street to Wendy's. Dee feeds him coffee and a bowl of chili that he wolfs down. He regales her with tales about how, when he was a kid, he fixed chili all the time because his father was never at home. He was either at work or chasing women.

"One lady that lived with us for a while taught me how to make chili. It's a trash meal because you can put anything in it. Chicken, hamburger, tofu, beans, vegetables, you name it. Whatever you have in the fridge."

"That's sounds interesting," she says, stifling a yawn.

"Am I boring you?"

"No, you're not boring me," she says, patting his knee. She moves her hand to his crotch and squeezes.

They head back to his house and trudge upstairs to the bedroom. He kicks off his shoes and drops his pants. When he jumps in the bed, the springs groan. He piles up three pillows, lies back, and sighs, "I'm sober."

"Yes, you are." His eyes are at half-mast, though open enough to see that Dee is positioning herself at the foot of the bed. He knows that he is about to experience an unveiling and waits in anxious anticipation, while at the same time thinking, for some unknown reason—probably the booze—

about once, when he was a teen, finding his father in bed with a woman. Dee unbuttons her blouse, exposing her milky flesh, unblemished except for a line of freckles that run along the right side of her ribcage like a quarter moon. He barely has time to take this in when she reaches behind her and unsnaps her bra. Her breasts fall out. She smiles and strolls around the side of the bed. Climbs in beside him.

"Why don't you take off your skirt?"

"Maybe I don't want you to see my legs." But Dee takes off her skirt and moves her legs up beside his. "They're not attractive."

He leans up on his elbows. "Yes, they are."

"You're not looking close enough. If I didn't shave for a couple of weeks, my legs would look like yours. Like if you only saw my legs, you'd think I was a man."

"Come on. That's crazy. I'm looking at you here almost completely naked," he says, pulling down her panties. She kicks them off. "Completely naked. You have a gorgeous body." He leans down, kisses her stomach, and moves his lips down farther. She runs her fingers through his hair. Moans. He looks up. "You see."

"Yes." She seems to have difficulty catching her breath. "When are you going to make love to me?"

"Right now." He pulls off his boxers and slides on top of her, nibbles her ear like a little mouse. She reaches down between his legs and yanks his pecker and, when it's hard enough, rams it inside her and rocks from side to side, driving it deeper. She wraps her legs around his back and gasps in his ear, "Harder, harder, harder." Mitch tries to accommodate her, but he feels somewhat undone. It seems to him that she is trying to lead the dance that he is supposed to lead, but it doesn't matter. It's comforting not to be in charge—as a matter of fact, to share the honors, like tag-team wrestlers. Besides, now he is thinking of what Gail suggested when they first made love, about distracting the mind in order to avoid premature ejaculation. But when he thinks of Gail, and he imagines that these are Gail's lips that he is kissing, he's suddenly on the verge of losing himself. Dee drags her fingernails down his back and wails in his ear like a diva. She buries his face in kisses, and he pumps her harder and harder as she insists, harder, harder. And then he remembers a chant he heard from the sidelines when he played football in high school. "Hit 'em again. Hit 'em again. Harder. Harder." He ejaculates.

"Oh-h-h-h," Dee gasps as her body tightens and toes curl up. She arches her back. "Oh-h-h, God. Marvelous. Marvelous."

She staggers to the bathroom to clean off. Mitch props the pillows behind his head and looks out the open window across the street at Wendy's. A white sedan pulls up to the drive thru. He can hear a man's voice ordering, followed by the static from the speakers and the hum of the traffic on New Hampshire. It is two in the morning. Mitch feels lonely. He just made love to a beautiful woman, and he feels lonely. He misses his kids. He misses Gail. He can understand her point of view, that she needs time to think things over. He should probably do some of that himself, not dwell on his hurt feelings. *But hey,* he thinks, remembering how he reacted when Kathy left him, *maybe I'm not that much different from Ed.*

He can hear Dee fumbling around in the bathroom. She clears her throat. Turns on the water. Sounds like she's brushing her teeth. A gentle wind blows back the curtains, curls around his toes, and runs up his legs like a woman's hand.

Dee wanders back into the room, hops in bed, and curls up next to him.

"What are you thinking?" she asks.

"Oh, I don't know. I'm thinking you're a very nice person, and I don't deserve you." In a twisted sense, Mitch means what he says. She is a "nice person," but only in the sense that he is not. He knows that she is the spider and he is the fly caught in her web. But the truth is, he doesn't mind being caught. He knows he will be able to wiggle free once he gets what he wants, and that's what makes him less of a "nice person."

She runs her hands through his hair. "That's a very nice thing to tell me," she says, "but you can't fool me. I'm not a shrinking violet."

"Of that I am sure," says Mitch, leaning closer and kissing her delectable, swanlike neck. "You're as tough as nails."

They make love again. This time she's on top, bouncing up and down, the springs of the bed groaning, him feeling like a hoppy ball with a handle that kids bounce up and down on at the playground. His mouth is open. He's squeezing his eyes shut. Oh, he could go on with this forever.

Afterward, Dee professes hunger and they drift downstairs to raid the refrigerator. Mitch lines up four pieces of whole-wheat bread on the counter. Slaps on mustard, mayo, lettuce, sliced ham, Swiss cheese, and pickles. He closes the sandwiches and roots around the kitchen cabinets until he comes up with a bag of Cool Ranch Doritos. Dee pops open two bottles of Corona. They head into the living room. Sit down on the couch.

They switch on the TV to the classic channel and watch a movie. Dee asks Mitch if he ever considered feature films as a career.

"Oh, I wouldn't mind getting into film, but I don't have the training."

"You could go to a film school," she says. She leans closer, puts her hand on his knee. "I've heard UCLA has a good one. Maybe you want to become a director. You stand a good chance, given your experience."

"I'd rather not go back to school," he says, playing along with her fantasy. "Maybe I'd work a few low-budget films as an independent and join the union after I earned my credentials. I had a friend did that."

"Yes, that would work," says Dee. "I've heard of many directors who start off working behind the camera."

"What makes you think I want to become a director?"

"I don't know. I thought you might be happier in a more exciting job," she says in a reticent voice. She seems a bit upset. "I mean, an exciting job in an exciting new place."

"That's true. I might be, if I could bring my children, but since I share custody with Kathy, I don't think so—though I had a friend who did exactly that, the same one who works in Hollywood. Now his kids are teenagers, and they barely know him. I don't want that to happen to me. Besides, why would you want me to move three thousand miles away? Would you come with me?"

"I would consider it, but I have so much to lose," she says. She can probably detect the uncertainty in his voice. "I mean, no, it's probably a bad idea for me, considering the cut in pay. L.A. is expensive. It's better for us to stay here."

He doesn't know what she means by "us," as if they are a couple on the verge of an important decision. He doesn't want to give her that impression.

They turn off the TV after their snack and rinse the dishes before they head off to bed. Mitch can sense that Dee wants to tell him something, but he doesn't want to hear it because then he'll have to say something back to her that she doesn't want to hear. He is dog-tired, but he can't fall asleep until he reasons things out. Mainly, he needs to tell Dee that it's all a mistake. He's not in love with her. She's a good friend. Things got out of hand. They had sex. It was great fun. She has a beautiful body. He would love to continue this, but with the understanding, you know, that it's not going anywhere. To Hollywood or anywhere else. Not even to living together. Or would it be more honorable to end it right now? *Sorry, Dee, it was great fun. You have a great body. You're great in bed. But I'm not in love with you. I'm in love with you know who, even though she has rejected me. I still hold out hope.* Or maybe he shouldn't tell her that he's in love with Gail. Spare her feelings. Say that he's doesn't want to get involved. To jump from one relationship to another. Maybe she'll understand, he thinks. Probably she won't. He falls asleep finally with the thought that maybe he's wrong. Maybe her feelings are as casual as his. Maybe this reference to Hollywood and all is a ploy to make him feel better, a fantasy to give substance to their lovemaking. Though this seems unlikely, it's the alternative he wants to believe.

Chapter Thirteen

It's the morning after the Stork Club party. Gail Strickland lies in bed after dropping Davy at the bus stop for school. She has nothing to do until her job starts in two weeks, a job Kathy helped her find at the American Psychological Association. Gail will edit the newsletter in addition to other "gopher" chores. It's a start.

She stares out the open window at an oak tree in the early blush of fall colors. A wind picks up and blows the leaves in her direction. They scatter in a red and yellow haze, and a few stick against the window screen. Gail feels the moist, chilly air wrap around her and pulls up the covers so that she's as warm as toast. She sighs. If only she could lie here forever drifting in and out of sleep, dreaming of what lies ahead: the new apartment in McLean Gardens, the easy walk to the Metro, the ride down to Union Station, the easy walk to the APA. Or perhaps she should live closer to the job in Capitol Hill or Penn Quarter, though she isn't as sure of the schools there as she is of the ones in Cleveland Park.

But for now she must climb out of bed to clean up around the house, as she promised Robin and Barry. They are at work. First she will clean the dishes that have been piled in the sink for the last two days. Then she will pick up the toys scattered over the floor like a minefield, then vacuum and mop where needed. The list of things to do is endless. Robin and Barry are slobs. They consider cleaning house optional, and Gail considers it a blessing that she can help out after all they have done for her.

The doorbell rings downstairs. Gail hurriedly dresses and runs down the steps. It's Ed. He's leaning casually against the porch rail holding twelve red roses. He grins out of the side of his mouth like a gangster. He thrusts the flowers in her direction when she opens a window beside the door.

"What do you want?" she asks.

"These are for you," he tells her. "I've come here to ask your forgiveness. It's all my fault, honestly. I'm to blame."

She warily opens the door and takes the roses. She puts them on the hall table.

Ed walks right into the house without being asked. Looks around. Laughs. "Those Spicers don't know how to keep a house clean like you do."

She doesn't know if this is intended as a compliment or not. She doesn't care. She asks him, what does he mean that he's to blame?

"I mean," he says in a low voice, as if he's not quite sure what to say next, "I mean, I let my emotions get the best of me, but that logically does not excuse my behavior. I know there was a reason you were having an affair. Maybe I wasn't paying enough attention to you. I don't know. But, in the end, what matters is that we resolve this problem so that we can both be happy. You know what I mean. I'm willing to take you back."

"Did you by any chance hear that I broke up with Mitch Lovett?"

"Yeah, I heard that, but I don't know if I believe it," he says, shifting his weight to the other foot, leaning closer, still grinning. "I'm willing to fight for you."

"Oh, you are," says Gail in a calm voice though underneath she's steaming. The nerve of the guy, she thinks.

"You bet. You're the most important person in my life, I've come to realize. I don't know how I could live without you."

"You should've thought of that before you slapped me around. Look here." She points at the bruise on her cheek.

He blushes, puts his hands in his pockets, and shrugs. "I'm truly sorry about that. I'm an emotional guy, especially when somebody betrays my trust."

She isn't paying much attention to what he's saying. They are excuses that aren't worthy of her sympathy. She has been taking his abuse for years. No longer.

"If Davy hadn't come in the room where we were fighting," she says, reminding him of when she left—what was it?—a month ago, "you would've taken that belt you picked up off the floor and beaten me to a pulp. If it's a matter of forgiving you, all right, I forgive you. But it's more than that."

Ed seems puzzled. His mouth is half open, as if the wheels in his tiny brain are grinding around and around trying to make connections. Suddenly, he wheels around and runs out the door. He digs in the backseat of the black Nissan truck and grabs a box, but her eyes fall upon the muzzle of one of his shotguns. It sticks out from under the seat like a pig's snout.

"Here, here," he yells as he thrusts the box in the air so she can see. Then he runs up the walk. Before he can push his way inside again, she slams the door and locks it.

"Now wait, wait, don't worry," he says on the other side, almost in a whimper, "I got you something that you will really like. I know you'll like it because once you told me you love emeralds."

"You bought me an emerald?" she asks through the door.

"Yes. Look." He opens the box and presses it against the window next to the door so that she can see. Inside is a small green pendant in the shape of a shamrock. She wonders if it's a real emerald or a piece of glass. She doesn't ask.

She opens the door, and he hands the box to her. She looks at the pendant carefully. "It's beautiful, the way the shamrock is surrounded by tiny cut diamonds."

"Yeah, I knew you would like it since you are half Irish and all," he says, smiling. His eyes seem to twinkle in the old way with the tiny crow's-feet that make them like miniature suns. *He is so gorgeous*, she thinks, but she doesn't weaken.

"Hey," he says, grabbing her arm too tightly, "I sold one of my favorite pieces at a gun show so I could buy this for you. I love you with all my heart."

Gail hands the box back to Ed. "It's really exquisite," she says, "but I can't take it."

He sits in a chair next to the hall table and breaths out hard, as if he's been sprinting for a long while. "May I have a glass of water?" he asks.

"Of course," she says. She pours some water out of the tap in the kitchen and takes it to him.

He is now in the living room sitting on the sofa, his elbows on his knees, staring down at the pendent in the box. He twists the box around so that the light in the stones reflects against his face. He puts the box on the coffee table. He gulps down the water and looks up at Gail. There are tears in his eyes.

"I know I haven't been a very good husband," he says, his voice cracking, "but I'll tell you what. Remember that session I told you about in Salt Lake, you know, the one about coaches who were former athletes? How they may have never dealt with what it was like to be out of the limelight? We're in shock. Like our life ended when we quit sports and now we have to create a new one."

"I've heard this story before," says Gail, crossing her arms in front of her chest. She feels sorry for him, but she felt that way many times and nothing changed, so why would anything change now?

"Now, listen. Now, listen," he begs, reaching out for her arm. She backs up. "Now, listen, when I returned from Salt Lake, I realized I hadn't started a new life outside of sports, so I resolved to do my darnedest. I mean, I took you out to a romantic comedy and a romantic dinner. Then I started to take out the trash and clean the dishes. I helped Davy build his little fort in the backyard and tossed the football with him. I even went dancing with you at Surf Club Live. You know how I hate dancing."

"Too little, too late," she says, her arms still crossed. She's staring at him now with an intensity that seems to bother him.

He wipes the tears from his eyes with the back of his hand and says, in a little boy's contrite voice, "I know it is. It's that I'm so much in love with you that I don't know what to do with myself now that you're gone."

"You can do what you were saying earlier. Start a new life." She is afraid, but his brows are furrowed in a puzzled expression that makes her think that he is listening to what she's saying. "What you need to do is improve yourself. What was wrong with our relationship is that you were angry all the time. You were like a tinderbox. Anything could set you off."

"You mean that I need something like anger-management classes," he says, nodding thoughtfully, though she backs off. Puts the coffee table between Ed and herself in case he decides to lunge at her. He does not take kindly to advice.

"You have a very strong point there," he says leaning forward on the couch and reaching over the coffee table until he touches the hem of her dress. He falls back, looks her straight in the eyes. "If I did that—maybe go into rehab for a year or so, I could learn ways of curbing my anger by, let's say, walking around the block a couple of times until I calmed down. Then, when I'm really better, we could live together, and if it works out we could make it a permanent arrangement."

"That's not what I mean. We're finished as a couple," says Gail, worried that this might set him off. "I mean, you get yourself right in the head. Then you go out and find another woman, if that's what you need. How about Dee Wynn? She's prettier than me."

"No, she isn't." He leans forward, puts his hands on his knees. He seems so nervous, like he's about to do something but can't figure out what. "Dee is pretty, but she thinks she's so smart. She'd drive me crazy. I need somebody like you, with a pleasant personality."

Now it's Gail's time to laugh. "I'm not that pleasant."

"Well, what I need is someone who isn't going to question everything I do."

She doesn't say anything. She stands there with her arms still crossed, as solid as rock.

"What I need is a person like you," he says, thoughtfully tapping his chin. "Listen, listen, I have an idea. Why not, after my rehab, we take a long vacation. We'll leave Davy with one of the Stork Club families, maybe Sonya's or Robin's, and head to wherever you want. Maybe travel around the world until we come to a place we like and settle down. We'll call for Davy and he'll travel over. We'll put him in an international school. Like, for instance, we settle in Madrid. I'll find a job with the Real Madrid as a coach. I know a lot about soccer."

"You can't speak Spanish."

"That doesn't matter. The Real Madrid is an international team—not to say that everyone in Europe knows English." He brightens, as if, by playing along, Gail is considering his views. "Besides, it doesn't have to be Madrid. It could be New Zealand. They have soccer teams and they speak English. What do you think?"

"You're clutching at straws," she says, trying not to smile because it was to New Zealand that she wanted to flee with Mitch, the possibility of which was as remote as her going to New Zealand with Ed.

"You're right," says Ed, standing up and shaking his head. He starts pacing the room. "I want to know one thing, though. Why is it that you will not come back to me after I go to rehab, if I actually prove to you that I am better, that I won't get angry anymore?"

"There's more to it than your anger."

"Yeah. Sure. What more is there?"

He stops pacing and glares at her in such a fierce way that she guesses that he is about to lose his temper. Her eyes come to rest on a poker by the fireplace. She pretends to be gathering her thoughts and wanders around the room until she comes to rest at the stand holding the fireplace tools. She whirls around.

"I don't know, Ed," she says, "your anger is only part of the problem. The other part is me, the way I am. I've taken abuse from you for years, and I haven't done a single thing about it until Mitch Lovett came along. Then I ran to him. It got me to thinking, I've been running from man to man since I left high school. That's why I broke up with Mitch. I think it would be totally dishonest of me to be with another man until I've gotten my own head together. Then I will be able to make a rational decision."

"What you are saying is that I still have a chance," he says, as the fierce look seems to melt from his face. "I mean, since I am the father of our child, the only rational decision is that you come back to me."

"That is not a rational decision," she says, moving her hand close to the poker so all she has to do is reach down in one swift movement. "It is not rational for me to return to a man who has abused me for years and nearly killed me when he found out I was having an affair."

"But, I will be a brand-new person when we get back together," he pleads, his hands in a prayerful position pointing toward her. He bends his legs. Is he about to get down on his knees? "I promise. I swear to God."

Gail can't hold back any more, she is so frustrated. "I don't love you anymore," she says. "As a matter of fact, I think I hate you."

Ed flinches as if he's been punched in the gut. He bends lower; his eyes squeezed half shut. He's in pain, she thinks, and she almost feels sorry for him. Then he grits his teeth and yells back at her. "You know how to hurt a person, don't you?"

"I'm not trying to hurt you," she says simply.

"But you are hurting me. You don't know how much I love you." He takes two steps in her direction.

"I don't care. I don't love you back," she says, taking hold of the poker.

He balls his fists and rears back as if he's about to slug her. Gail brandishes the poker in his face. "Don't you come closer," she says, full of adrenaline that makes her dizzy. "I'll kill you."

She means it. He hesitates, his mouth agape as he stares at the pointy end of the poker. He checks around the room, as if in search of a weapon with which to defend himself. She takes a few steps forward. He backs off, trips over one of the toys scattered on the floor, and falls down. He scuttles back toward the door as she trudges toward him with a fierce determination. The poker is over her head. She would love dearly to smash it down on his, but she doesn't.

Ed grabs the doorknob. Jumps to his feet. He checks over his shoulder. She catches a glimpse of fear in his eyes, and it makes her feel good. For once, he's the one who's afraid.

He flings open the door and flees to his pickup.

When Gail realizes that he might be after his shotgun, she drops the poker. She slams the door closed and locks it and then looks out the window. Ed is in the driver's seat staring back at her. Though the fear has gone from his eyes, his mouth is still agape. He slams the truck into gear, peels off down the street, and, as if in afterthought, throws Gail the bird.

She wanders over to the couch. Her legs are shaking. Her stomach is queasy. She sits down heavily. She doesn't cry; maybe years ago that's how she would react, but not now. She is, as a matter of fact, pleased with herself. Like she knows now what it feels like to look out of Ed's eyes into her own. It gives her a sense of power that he must've felt all these years. Not that her feeling would last. Ed could overpower her whenever he wished. He harbors a relentless anger that she lacks.

She needs to think. She can't spend the rest of day cleaning the house now—Ed might come back, and this time he might use the shotgun he has stashed in the backseat. She has to go out among people, where he would less likely harm her. She grabs her coat and heads up Hickory, pausing at Savory. The restaurant is across from the school-bus stop. She'll come back here at three to grab Davy before Ed does. There's no telling what he has in mind.

She wanders down Laurel to Old Town, feeling disoriented until she climbs the front steps to Amano, a lady's shop in a stucco foursquare where they carry the hippie-chic items that she loves. She wanders around the store fingering the clothes on the racks. She relaxes. She's in her element. Shopping, though she has no money—it's enough to make her feel like she has returned to a modicum of sanity. She stops at the shoes and picks up a pair of lime-green flats that look familiar. She checks at the brand name—Arcopedico, shoes for the active woman. She turns the shoe around in her hand. Her eyes alight on another pair, yellow ones, and suddenly she remembers. Years ago, she and Ed were on vacation in New Orleans, before Davy was born. She left the exact same yellow shoes behind there. They were comfortable, like walking on air, and they complimented most of her informal outfits. She wanted to buy another pair, but Ed refused. He wanted to teach her a lesson about frugality, and, since she had quit her job, she had no money. The lesson took hold. She throws the lime-green flats back onto the display table, knocking over the yellow pair. They clatter to the floor. The salesperson behind the desk looks up and frowns. Gail picks up the shoes, puts them back carefully, and scurries out of the shop.

She hurries up the street past the town gazebo and the statue of Roscoe the Rooster, who was the town greeter five years ago, before he was squashed by a truck. She slows to a walk, tip-toes into the S&A bead store, where she gazes at the jewelry in the display cases and thinks about fashioning her own, though it's not her passion. She would rather own a Bakelite bracelet or an extravagant art deco piece dripping with phony diamonds and sapphires. She wonders if the emeralds in the shamrock pendant Ed purchased are real. It's probably cheap green glass of some sort. That's the way she feels, like a cheap imitation—the bravado she showed in front of Ed was just that, cheap bravery with no substance behind it. She yearns right now more than anything in the world to flee into Mitch's arms wherever he might be—on a shoot, in his house. It doesn't matter. He would protect her. She slogs down Laurel toward the bus stop and, when she turns the corner, sees Larry and Davy bouncing up and down on the sidewalk like jackrabbits. Suddenly, her resolve returns.

She rushes up to her son and his friend. They stop their jumping to stare at her. They beg for ice cream cones at Savory.

"Sure, sure," she says. This fits into her plans. She drags them across the street and sits in the back of the restaurant while they slurp the ice cream out of their cones. She sips a latte and stares nervously out the window.

"What you looking for?" Davy asks her.

"Nothing."

"Is Daddy coming by?"

"Of course not. What makes you think so?"

"I don't know. You seem scared."

They wait for another few minutes until Robin Spicer races in, out of breath. "Oh, I totally forgot about Larry," she says. "I was about to take Ruth to ballet when all hell broke loose."

She leans down and whispers in Gail's ear. "Barry was over at Wendy's picking up a couple of cheeseburgers after work when he saw two cop cars race up Oak Lane to Mitch Lovett's house. He saw Ed's black Nissan pickup parked out front. Then he called me on the cell to say that he's going to check out what's up as soon as things settle down."

Chapter Fourteen

The sun pours in the window, blinding Dee Wynn as she opens her eyes. She turns on her side. She feels cold and curls up closer to Mitch. He doesn't stir. He's a deep sleeper, or maybe he's not asleep at all. She resists the desire to poke him; they haven't slept more than seven hours. She reaches down to the floor, where she finds her purse and pulls out her cell. It is next to the full pack of cigarettes—full minus the one that she smoked the night she found out that Mitch was screwing Gail. *How time flies*, she thinks, smiling with a sense of fulfillment. She texts on the cell that she won't be in for work today, but definitely early on Tuesday. The other partners trust her. She will spend the day with Mitch, but she'll let him sleep for now.

She slips out of bed and tiptoes to the bathroom. She takes a long, hot shower. The pipes bang like drums. Mitch needs to fix up this place. Install copper pipes for one, new flooring for another, and probably plenty of other things. It's not worth the effort.

She lets her mind float freely as the water flows in tiny, steamy rivulets down the angles of her body. She feels this nervous energy inside her that reminds her of the energy she feels when she's nearing the completion of a project. She'd look down at the drawing and up at the project, the gold leaf in the ceiling of the atrium at Union Station, for instance, and inside her she'd know it was a matter of time. She soaps herself up. Twists around until she's rinsed off. With Mitch as well, it's only a matter of time until she'll have him in the palm of her hand. She giggles like a teenager then turns off the water, wraps a towel around her, and tiptoes back into the bedroom. Mitch is leaning back against a pile of pillows with his hands behind his head, staring at the ceiling, and then at her.

"Good morning," he says.

"Good morning." She lets the towel drop so he can see her body, even her legs. She is no longer self-conscious in front of him.

"You're very beautiful," he says.

"Thank you." She slips into bed next to him. He looks at her body for a long moment in a hungry way, as if she is a lamb ready for slaughter. Then he turns away.

She laughs nervously, feeling the chilly air blowing through the open window. The sun drifts in and out of dark clouds, casting shadows over the room. She pulls up a blanket. "Why did you purchase this house?" she asks, trying to stave off the negative thoughts that are leaking into her brain for no reason she can think of. Maybe the way he reacted to what she said last night.

"To be near my children," he says, turning back to her, his eyes on her breasts, which she has kept uncovered. He reaches over and pulls the blanket up to her chin. "You must be freezing."

"Oh, I guess I am a little cold," she says, catching herself nervously twisting her hair around her finger like her mother. "Kathy told me once that you're good at investments, so what I'm thinking is that this house must also be an investment."

"You're thinking right," he says turning toward her on his side and leaning on his elbow. He tells her about how the land he owns is zoned commercial and one of the chain hardware stores is interested in buying. "I don't own all the land, but enough to squelch the deal unless I agree. Gives me leverage."

"You're a smart man, Mitch," she says, brushing the hair out of his eyes, though she doesn't want to give the impression that she's fawning in any way.

He grabs her wrist gently. "Listen, Dee, I was drunk last night, and I don't want to give you the wrong idea, but..."

"But what?"

"But I don't want to take advantage of you. I don't want you to think things that aren't true. I want you to understand my feelings toward you."

"Oh, I understand perfectly," says Dee who doesn't understand at all though she pretends she does because she doesn't want this to wreck her plans. "I understand that, at the start of a relationship, it's scary because you don't know how it's going to end up."

"I don't know if *relationship* is the correct word to use in this case, Dee. We've been friends for years, and I don't want that to end. Maybe the sex is getting in the way."

"I can handle that," says Dee, though she's not sure she can. "I think we are friends having sex. I think we are definitely attracted to each other. I don't know on what level, whether it's superficial or deeper, but I want to find out."

"You know I'm on the rebound."

"Yes, I know."

"You know I'm still in love with Gail."

"Yes, I know." She is beginning to feel cheap, like she's second best, or not even that.

"But I am really, truly attracted to you. There are very few women that are as beautiful and as smart as you are."

"Brains and beauty too." She laughs, runs her hand down his cheek gently. "But don't worry. I'm not in love with you either. I'm infatuated. But not in love, you know, like in a more or less permanent way."

"Yes, my feelings exactly," says Mitch with a sigh of relief. "Then we have a perfect understanding that this isn't going anywhere."

"Yes," says Dee though that's not what she said. It's what he said, and that makes a world of difference. She thinks about the difference for a moment and excuses herself. She has to go to the bathroom. She catches the look of concern on his face as she closes the bathroom door tightly and then turns on the sink faucet. It's a trick the nuns taught her at Little Flower to keep boys from hearing girls tinkle. She sits on the toilet and bursts out in silent sobs. It's not true, what she said—she is in love. Madly, forlornly, irretrievably, like she has never been before.

But she has to analyze this like she analyzes all her relationships, and after the tears stop, she comes to the conclusion that she has never truly been rejected before. It was she who did the rejecting just as she had with Bob Johnson. This is a totally new experience, and, as with all new experiences, she must approach the situation with caution. She knows that this too is an act of will. If she wants to live a reasonable life, she has to keep in control of herself, she thinks as she looks at her red eyes in the mirror. How will she explain that? She grabs a few tissues, opens the door, and feels her way down the hallway to the bedroom, blinking.

"What's wrong?" asks Mitch, sitting up. "You've been gone a long time."

"I got something in my eyes this morning when I was taking a shower. I hope it isn't a piece of metal from your pipes." She leans close to him. He looks in her eye. Takes the tissue from her. He pokes around gingerly and, after a few minutes, comes out with a spec, probably mascara.

"I got it," he says, showing it to her. "But I don't think it's metal. Maybe dirt."

He checks the other eye but can find nothing. She blinks several times, shakes her head.

"You got it all."

"Good."

Her face is close to his. Her breasts are against his bare chest, but she doesn't make the first move. She is too proud after all that he has said to her. When he sweeps her up in his arms and gently pulls her down to the bed, she feels gratified. Her resolve returns, though with a caveat. She may not win him over today. She may not win him over tomorrow. It may take her months, but she will win him over eventually, and he will forget that Gail Strickland ever existed.

She is thinking this as they are making love, and it redoubles her passion. It seems to work on his as well; after their final passion rolls into the station, he rolls off of her. "Oh, Jesus," he moans.

"Oh, brother," she moans.

They lie there for a long moment relaxing until Dee remembers the cigarette pack. She pulls it out of her purse. "You want one?"

"Sure, why not," says Mitch, taking the pack from her. He takes out two cigarettes and the matches from behind the cellophane. He puts the cigarettes between his lips and lights both. He hands one to Dee. "I saw that in a film noir a couple of days ago. Probably French."

"You know why the French smoke in bed after they make love?" she asks, remembering a joke she heard a long time ago, probably from one of her French clients. "They need to relax before they go home to see their wives."

"Very funny," says Mitch in a weak chortle.

"Yes, very funny," says Dee, feeling uncomfortable. She fluffs up the pillow and lies back. Mitch empties the coins from a bowl on the side table, and they use it as an ashtray. She checks the room out, as if seeing it for the first time. It is somewhat untidy, but not to the extent of Robin and Barry Spicer's house. They are legendary slobs. Mitch's room is cluttered, but in an organized way. In one corner, there's a pile of books; in another, a pile of tools and a hamper; and on one wall, on top of a long table, his camera equipment. There is a framed illustration on the wall above the table that seems puzzling. It is of a man in a black cape and top hat. He wears a white mask and smokes a cigarette. The illustration is professionally done. The man is very handsome. He looks like Mitch.

Dee flicks the cigarette ashes in the bowl. Coughs. She takes another pull. "Is that you?" She points at the illustration.

"Oh, no, that's my father," he says, snickering as if embarrassed.

"It's amazing, the resemblance."

"Yes, but I hope it's only skin deep," says Mitch, flicking some ashes in the bowl and coughing as well. "This is disgusting," he says, stamping out the cigarette. "Now I know why I quit." He waves his hands in the air to disperse the smoke.

"What do you mean by skin deep?" She puts out her cigarette and lies back.

"I mean my father was a jerk and I don't want to be like him and now I am."

"You'd rather still be with Kathy."

"You're getting a little too personal, Dee," he laughs, fretfully. "Yes, I wish we never broke up, but we did, and that's that."

She's not sure if she likes these pat answers, but she feels like she's getting somewhere. "I mean, it seems like an obvious question, but why do you want to be with her? Do you still love Kathy?"

"After fourteen years of marriage, I don't think that's something you get over. But that's in the past. My kids are not. Everyone thinks that kids are resilient. That's a lie." He raises his voice. *Is he angry?* wonders Dee. He's normally such an even-tempered guy—that's one of the reasons she likes him.

"I know from experience that kids are not resilient. Like me, for instance. I moved from place to place, school to school, friend to friend, mother to mother, if you know what I mean. You can only stretch a rubber band so far before it breaks."

"You seem to have come out of it all right."

"Only because my father was a very good teacher. Whatever he did, I do the opposite. But not every kid is like me. I'm not sure that I'm like me. Maybe I'll break," he says laughing fretfully again.

Dee gets it. He is a dedicated father. Maybe she should appeal to him on that level. But not yet. He is too tied down to the old life—Kathy, the family, the possibility of Gail—to embark on a new one. But there will come a day.

She watches him as he jumps out of bed into a pair of weathered jeans with holes in the knees. He pulls on a Cayman Island T-shirt. She remembers when they vacationed in the Caymans together. Jack Fucker was there. They stayed in a condo on the beach and one day she and Jack swam as far as they dared, to the edge of the Cayman Trench, and dove for conch shells. Dee remembers how frightened she was peering into the darkness of the trench. She swam ashore as fast as she could when she saw a sand shark fan itself in the cold currents. Jack thought she was funny. They were in the first blush of their love affair. She remembers the feeling, and it flares up again, only a thousand times stronger as she watches Mitch hop from foot to foot, pulling on his slippers.

He sits down on the edge of the bed. She runs her hand across his chest, feels the tight, ropey muscles. She tweaks his nipple. He jumps. "Not now. I'm hungry."

She pushes him down. He reaches for her breast dangling above his hand. She jumps aside and rolls out of bed.

"I think I'm hungry too." She slips into a pair of shorts that hang from the bedpost and pulls a T-shirt over her head. "I hope you don't care if I wear your clothes. I don't want to get all dressed up."

"That's fine," he says, a puzzled expression on his face.

"I'll go downstairs to rustle up brunch. You relax. Take a shower or something. We'll have breakfast in bed."

"Hey, that's great."

She waves good-bye and turns to leave but senses his eyes upon her and turns back. Their eyes meet. She thinks she senses a longing in his eyes, and that satisfies her. She has made progress today, she thinks. Time is on her side. She drifts out of the room to the stairs. An uneasy feeling grips her, but she shakes it off. She creeps slowly down the stairs, and on the third step down, the front door crashes open. She freezes. A shaft of light pours across the threshold to the stairs. She can see someone step inside. She can see a pair of black boots and the frayed cuffs of a pair of jeans. She notices the sunshine and the dust motes that drift between her and the disembodied figure on the floor below. She is about to say something when she hears a metallic click that sounds like shack-a-lack. It is an unfamiliar but somehow sinister sound. She feels cold as ice.

"Who," she inquires in a whisper that is probably too low for the disembodied figure to hear, but before she can inquire any further, she sees a hot tongue of orange flame like a dragon's breath reach out to her. Her arm catches fire. The banister next to her hand is torn to splinters. Another shack-a-lack. The wall to her right explodes and covers her with dust. She turns to flee, loses her balance, and levitates in thin air like an angel without wings.

Chapter Fifteen

When their eyes meet as she leaves the room, Mitch Lovett is thinking about how he uses women to make him feel better. Didn't Gail say that? And wasn't he now using Dee just as he had before, when Kathy divorced him? To make love to a woman you don't love—doesn't that make you a total loser? Doesn't that make him exactly like his father? He feels that his father is in the room laughing at him—the randy old cad—but this feeling only lasts a second, until the front door bangs open. He hears footsteps, followed by a metallic click, and Dee Wynn whispering, "Who?" She sounds like an owl hooting in the forest behind his house.

He scrambles up from the bed, sees a flash of light followed by a deafening roar, and the sound of splintering wood. Dee screams. He tries to scramble back before he reaches the door and grabs the doorjamb only to see another flash of light, but he does not hear the roar because his brain is occupied with a searing pain that climbs up his forearm to his chest. He falls backward into the room, gritting his teeth. Dee topples down the stairs. Her body whacks against a solid object. He can't tell what—the newel post? Did she hit her head against the newel post? Oh, Jesus. He can hear her body crumple to the floor at the bottom of the stairs.

Mitch's arm is on fire, and he could easily give in to the pain, but he knows his life depends on what he does next. He rushes to the closet and pulls down the metal box. It falls open when it bangs to the floor. He hears a voice from below.

"Holy shit. It's fucking Dee."

He opens the box of .38s. They clatter against the wood floor. He bends down. Feels the pain roar up his arm and nearly blacks out. He collapses to his knees, but then reaches over, picks up the bullets carefully, and slips them into the chamber one by one.

Mitch crawls over to a corner of the room where he can't be easily seen from the door. He pushes the hamper aside and leans against the wall. His whole body is shaking. He takes a few short breaths. His heart feels like it's going to pop out of his chest and run off down the road. He lifts the weapon slowly and aims it at the door, waiting for the footsteps on the stairs. They don't come.

That's when he hears the shack-a-lack of the gun followed by another explosion, three times over until his ears are ringing. Then he hears a voice yelling, "Mitch Lovett, I know you're up there. You cock-sucking Cajun son of a bitch, you bung-holing, shit-faced, lily-livered, numb-nutted, wasted, lying, wife-stealing, back-stabbing son of a..."

Ed Strickland doesn't finish his sentence because he chokes up. Mitch can hear him start to cry. He fires off another round, and after the deafening roar echoes through the house, he screams in anguish, "So you're fucking Dee, so you're fucking my wife, so you just want to fuck everything like you're a fucking dog that doesn't know no better. Well, now you're fucking with me, you fucking son of a bitch. Come on down here right now so I can blow your sorry-assed brains out."

But Mitch won't budge. As sorry assed as he might feel, he knows he doesn't stand a chance against a shotgun, as Ed's gun must surely be, judging from the pellets lodged in his arm. A pump action of some sort that would reduce him to pieces of stringy flesh splattered against a wall before he is able to fire off a single shot.

He stands a better chance where he is, a chance to get a jump on Ed. Ed, though, seems more intent on stomping around downstairs from room to room yelling about how he's going to find Gail. She's hiding somewhere, he yells. Mitch can hear him rummaging through the kitchen and living room, knocking over furniture. Maybe she climbed out the window, Ed cackles, and is running around the woods naked, the fucking cunt. He fires off a couple more shots. Comes to the foot of the stairs.

"Hey, you up there," he screams, "you chicken-hearted jerk ass. I know you're up there. Where is my frigging wife? I know you know where she is. Hiding under your bed, maybe. I'm coming up after you."

He pumps his gun. Fires up the stairwell. Hits the back wall. Plaster chunks fly in the bedroom followed by a cloud of dust that settles on Mitch's bed. Ed pumps again and fires. He creeps up the stairs. He is a one-man demolition team. "Here I come," he yells. "I'm fucking coming."

Mitch is amazed at how calm he is. The pain in his arm has gone away, a throbbing numbness in its place. His mouth is dry. He focuses on the door, his mind totally intent on what is about to happen, like a golfer about to make a shot. Mitch imagines the muzzle of Ed's shotgun poking through the bedroom door. He's in the front left-hand corner of the room. He lifts the thirty-eight and blows a hole in Ed's shoulder. Ed is thrown against the wall. Mitch blasts three more holes in his chest. Ed's eyes roll up in his head. He slides down to the floor in a heap, leaving a blood smear down the wall behind him.

Only this isn't the way it happens, because halfway up the stairs, Ed Strickland creeps to a halt, as if he forgot something. He mumbles to himself. Mitch can't hear what he's saying, but he can distinctly hear a clicking sound. Like pieces of metal clicking together. Ed is reaching in his pocket for shells. He is loading his shotgun. Mitch could right at this moment jump up. Run to the door. Point the thirty-eight down the stairs and shoot Ed Strickland before he has a chance to react. But he doesn't. He can't be 100 percent sure about the clicking sounds. It could be a ploy, like a duck call. Maybe Ed is trying to flush Mitch out of his safe place to get a clear shot at him.

Then there is a tiny pinprick of sound far off that changes this cat and mouse game, at least as far as Ed is concerned. It turns to a whine, like a lawn mower sputtering to life. It is a police car siren wailing, followed by two more wails coming from another direction.

"Oh, hell," Ed groans. He wheels around and stomps to the bottom of the stairs. Opens the front door and slams it shut behind him.

Mitch peers out the window and sees Ed dressed in jeans, a black T-shirt, and a hunter's vest. The shotgun is tucked under his arm, and he is scurrying toward the black Nissan. Across the street he sees a Lincoln Town Car, the windows rolled up, a Boston terrier inside jumping from seat to seat barking viciously, showing its teeth.

Mitch runs to the head of the stairs. Looks down and sees Dee. Her legs are on the stairs, one on top of the other, her body twisted sideways on the floor, her head turned away from him. He can see a black bruise on the back of her neck. Puncture wounds in one of her arms and in her side. Blood is seeping from the wounds, soaking the T-shirt of his that she's wearing. He bolts down the stairs and jumps over her body. He pulls open the door. He lifts the thirty-eight and points it at Ed's back as he hustles around the rear of his Nissan, empty-handed after tossing the shotgun in the truck bed. All Mitch has to do is pull the trigger like he imagined upstairs: a hole here, a hole there, a hole between the eyes.

Ed opens the driver's side door and then looks up to see Mitch aiming the gun at his chest. He jumps back, a startled look on his face, trips over a root, and falls down. Mitch can no longer see him. He wonders if Ed's going to creep around the side of the car and charge him like the football player he used to be. But he doesn't do that. He opens the car door instead. His head pops up behind the steering wheel. He turns over the engine, and the Nissan jerks off down Oak Lane, gathering speed. Mitch drops his arm and then the thirty-eight. It clunks against the cement porch.

A cop car races down Oak Lane and comes to a screeching halt, blocking the Nissan. Ed slams into the car—this only bends a fender, but it startles the cops long enough that he can jump out, race around the back of his truck, leaning low to make himself a small target, and dive into the woods. Two cops climb out of the vehicle, check the damage, and look into the woods where Ed disappeared. One of them goes around the back of the Nissan. He looks down in the truck bed and yells at the other, words Mitch can't hear. Then they both back off to the side of the road. And, as if on cue, four other police cars top the hill, brakes squealing and rubber burning. All the cops jump out of their cars. There must be ten of them. They confer with the first two on the scene, draw their guns, and race into the woods.

Mitch Lovett watches all this with a sense of unreality, like he's filming a scene behind his camera. Only this time, all his senses are engaged. Especially touch. Pain. Upstairs he felt a throbbing numbness, but down here, intense pain. The chills. His teeth are chattering. He looks down at his arm, which is covered in streaks of blood pouring out of maybe a dozen tiny holes. Some of the pellets he can see—they look like shiny gray eyeballs. Others burrowed deeper, broke the bone above his wrist. His hand is swelling. He feels like he's going to pass out but snaps to when he sees two policemen emerge from the woods dragging Ed between them.

They throw him up against one of the cop cars. Frisk him. The other cops emerge from the woods in pairs or groups of three. Mitch waves at the two closest to him and then staggers back inside his house and collapses on the floor next to Dee. He leans against the newel post. Outside, he glimpses the dapper old man in a cravat, the one with a thin salt-and-pepper mustache, open the door to his Lincoln Town Car. The Boston terrier jumps out. He puts a leash on the dog. They stand in front of the car, staring at him. A crowd gathers. A police car weaves through the Jiffy Wash lot, followed by an ambulance.

Mitch looks down at Dee. Her eyes are open. Not like eyes he has ever seen before on a living person—maybe mannequin eyes, maybe one of Addie's Barbie doll's eyes, like that of a life-sized Barbie lying in a broken heap at the bottom of the stairs. Mitch reaches over. Touches Dee's cheek. Still warm.

Two medics rush in the door. One is a short, skinny fellow with a wisp of a goatee. He bends down on one knee next to Dee. He doesn't want to soil his pants in her blood, thinks Mitch. The medic reaches out to check the pulse in her neck, then her wrist, then a few other spots where Mitch wasn't aware a pulse exists.

He glances up at a cop framed by the doorway, his hand on his holster. Is Mitch a suspect? His brain isn't functioning very well.

He looks back at the medics. The skinny one tells the other, a burly man with bugged-out eyes, that there's nothing they can do for Dee Wynn. He gestures at her with his thumb.

"She's dead."

Mitch covers his face, but he's unable to cry—the pain is too excruciating. He glances up at the medics imploringly. The burly medic picks up a red metal suitcase with a white cross on the side, lays it down beside Mitch, and opens it. He peers inside at the shiny needles, scissors, knives, saw, the Band-Aids, gauze, and whatnot. The skinny one pulls out a needle and flicks it a couple of times to eliminate air bubbles. He pokes Mitch in the arm. Morphine, he says. Mitch remembers only one thing after that, Barry Spicer peering over the shoulder of the bug-eyed medic. Barry seems to be crying. This upsets Mitch. He tries to sooth his friend, but the words that come out of his mouth are incoherent. It's like he's at the bottom of a well yelling up at Barry, who is at the top of the well but moving farther and farther away.

Chapter Sixteen

Mitch Lovett pokes his finger under the cast and tickles his itchy skin. Dry flakes come out under his fingernails. He feels like he's shedding. He is on the fifth floor of the Crowne Plaza. He doesn't ever want to return home, though the police will be taking down the crime tape tomorrow. It's been a week since Dee's death, three days since the funeral. He wanted to attend, but Kathy said it would disturb the family. Gail wasn't going. Kathy visited him in the hospital. Gail didn't, though she left a message on his cell. "It is my fault," she said. "I rushed over as fast as I could to your house that day when Dee told me about sleeping with you. I was full of jealousy. I forgot my family and thought of my own desires. You. Only you."

Mitch peers out the window of his room at the open court of the Crowne Plaza. He catches a glimpse of the divorced men sitting at the elevated bar surrounded by their kids. The kids are playing miniature golf. Watching TV. A few in bathing suits soak themselves under the indoor waterfall.

His cell rings. It's Dr. Wynn asking Mitch to lunch tomorrow at her house. Mitch doesn't have the slightest idea why Dee's mother would want to see him, considering the circumstances, but he accepts the invitation and promises to be there at one.

When Mitch finishes talking to Dee's mom, he snaps the cell closed and heads out of the room. Punches the elevator button. The elevator lurches down to the lobby. He wants to sit with the divorced men, listen to their stories. He needs to be distracted, unlike the last time he was here, with Addie and Julian.

He sits next to a man in a rumpled suit jacket who's talking to a bald man about how he dropped his daughter off at Dulles

Airport. "Her mother moved to Greensboro, North Carolina. Before, when she lived in Washington, I saw her once every other weekend, and on alternate holidays I'd take her up to my folks' in Connecticut. But now I'm lucky if I see Patty every other month."

"Why don't you move to Greensboro?" asks Mitch.

The man in the rumpled jacket turns to Mitch. "I thought about doing that, but, you know, it's far away, and there's no guarantee my ex will stay there."

The bald man inches closer. "I've seen you around here. You have two kids. But I don't see them here tonight."

"They're with their mother," says Mitch.

"So I guess you came here just for the hell of it," says baldy.

"Yeah. Sure."

"Like Barney, here." He points at the man in the rumpled suit. "He just can't stay away from his fellow divorced buddies."

"We're a kind of club," says Barney. "Want to join? All it takes is for your butt to get kicked out of the house you bought and paid for. Except for Stevie down there, whose wife makes more money than he does. That's *why* he got kicked out."

Stevie, a lantern-jawed man at the end of the bar, grins sheepishly.

"What's your poison?" asks the bartender.

"Try the single-malt scotch," says baldy. "Give him the list, Billy."

The bartender shoves a piece of paper in front of Mitch. He looks down at the names: Glenfiddich, Glenlivet, Macallan, Dalwhinnie, Oban, Laphroaig.

"My advice," says baldy, "is to start at the top and work your way down. Now, you and Barney can afford to. Me and Stevie, we got kids here."

"Okay, Glenfiddich," says Mitch.

"Neat or ice?" asks the bartender.

"Neat," says baldy.

"Neat," says Mitch. The bartender pours the drink in a small glass. Mitch takes a couple of sips.

"Good," he says, polishing off the first drink. He asks for the Glenlivet while listening to the stories of his newfound buddies. They are now whining about the apartments they live in and how their child-support payments are draining their cash reserves.

"I'll never be able to buy another house," says baldy.

Mitch gets as far as the Macallan and orders a Coke.

"What's the matter, man?" asks Barney who's already down at Laphroaig and starting over again. "Don't want to ruin your pretty face?"

"Yeah, that's it exactly."

"What's your story, anyway? You join our club you got to tell us," says Barney who is beginning to slur his words. His eyes are at half-mast.

"You don't want to hear it."

"Sure, we do," says baldy, leaning forward on his elbow. He's drinking Coke like Mitch. "I mean why do you have your arm in a cast? Did your wife beat you with a baseball bat or something?"

"No, that's not what happened at all," says Mitch, realizing why he is really down here. Not to hear them spill their guts, but to spill his own. So he starts at the hospital and works back to his house. The shotgun blasts. Dee toppling down the stairs. And then he explains how this all came to pass. How he found himself in this horrible situation.

"You mean to say," says Barney whose eyes are no longer at half-mast, "this guy broke into your house thinking you were screwing his wife and it was actually this other woman you were screwing and he blows her away by mistake?"

"Yes."

"Were you screwing his wife?"

"Yes, but we'd broken up."

"Unbelievable."

"But true," says Stevie. "I read an article in the *Washington Post* about it."

"No shit," says baldy, laughing. "No end of trouble a divorced man can get into if he puts his mind to it."

They all laugh. Go back to discussing their own situations. Baldy again decries his poverty. "I understand deadbeat dads. I mean, how would you feel if you had to turn your money over to a woman who hates your guts? And on top of that, you don't even get to live in your house and you barely see your kids."

Barney says it's worse for him. Especially the kid part, and that maybe Mitch is right—he should move to Greensboro, and if she moves out of Greensboro, he'll follow the bitch wherever she goes. He doesn't trust the woman after what she did to Patty. "Put her on Ritalin. Says that the teacher sent her to the school psychologist, who said that the divorce probably triggered her ADHD. Bullshit. The reason she's on Ritalin is that the teacher can't control her. Her mother said she's fine at home, but her mother is such an idiot she'll believe what any so-called professional tells her."

"You know what?" says Stevie, leaning toward Mitch. "I can understand why that fellow wanted to kill you. My wife was having an affair with her boss, or at least that's what I think. What I'd like to do is walk in on them fucking, and I'd say, 'Howdy, you know me.' And, when they did recognize me and their eyes got totally big, I'd blow their heads off."

"Jesus, Stevie," says the bald man. "Don't talk that way. You'd never be able to get away with it."

The next day Mitch drives slowly east through the park— first Rock Creek, then Sligo—trying to wrap his mind around what is about to transpire at Dr. Wynn's house. He knows mothers. He was married to one. They're all the same when it comes to defending their children. He takes a right on Sherman and parks his beat-up Saab in front of the doctor's bungalow. He climbs the stairs slowly and rings the bell.

Dr. Wynn swings open the door as if she's been anxiously waiting behind it for his appearance. "Mitch Lovett," she says somberly, taking his hand and squeezing it. "I'm glad you came. I know it must be difficult."

Mitch agrees that it is difficult. Says he is very sorry about Dee. And about what happened and why. That he feels a definite burden. "Not that I'm responsible necessarily, but I feel like I should have known better…"

"I appreciate your candor," says the doctor. She grabs him by the elbow and ushers him to a couch in front of a roaring fire. On the coffee table is a plate piled with finger sandwiches, as well as one bowl of potato chips and another of carrots and celery and dip. On a silver tray are two pots and cups and saucers.

"Tea or coffee?" asks Dr. Wynn.

"Tea."

"Cream and sugar."

"Splenda, if you have it."

Dr. Wynn reaches in the pocket of the smock she is wearing and pulls out a yellow packet. She pours the contents in his tea, stirs it with a spoon, and hands him the cup. Her lips are compressed. A woman on the far side of middle age. Salt-and-pepper hair. Soft eyes that wander over him like she's inspecting one of her patients. She pours herself a cup of coffee, sits back.

"Please, help yourself," she says, gesturing at the sandwiches. Mitch picks up a small plate and fishes for a sandwich—a ham and cheese—and three potato chips, carrots, and celery. He balances the plate on his knee while he sips the tea. He feels like he's at the Mad Hatter's tea party.

"Call me Bev," she says as she reaches for one of the sandwiches.

"Okay, Bev." He pokes one of the carrots in the dip. He is feeling extremely clumsy trying to balance everything with one arm in a sling.

"There is nothing a doctor appreciates in a patient more than candor," she says, smiling as he drops one of the carrots on the floor. She picks it up and puts it on the table. "How else can we make a proper diagnosis?"

"I'm not sure where you're headed with this, Bev," says Mitch as he swallows one of the sandwiches and munches on a potato chip. He wipes his fingers. He feels like a bug under glass.

"I want to show you something and I want you to be totally honest in your assessment. I assume you knew my daughter very well."

"I've known her for years."

"In a way that I would not know her. There's a lot she has not revealed to me. But here, I want to take you upstairs." She grabs his arm, and, as she pulls him up like an invalid from the couch, the plate balanced on his knee clatters to the floor.

"Oh, I'm sorry," she says. He helps her pick up the mess. "I'm so beside myself I don't know what to do. Three years ago my husband died, and I was coming to terms with that when this happened. How can you ever come to terms with your child dying before you, and in such a violent way?"

"You can't." He didn't mean to be so frank, but he was thinking of his own children and understood just how bad she must feel.

She looks at him for a moment, as if she's been stung by a slap. "More candor," she says, taking his hand and pulling him upstairs to Dee's old bedroom. She leads him over to a vanity table. Snatches up a pink envelope. Opens it. Pulls out a piece of paper. Unfolds it and thrusts it in Mitch's face. "Read this," she demands.

"I know what it says."

"Okay, then." She drops her hand. The paper drops to the floor. He looks down at the paper, open so he can see all the letters printed on the page especially the FUCKING, which stands out like a cruel reminder of what he's been up to. He looks up at Dr. Wynn—he can't think of her as Bev—who is giving him a scrutinizing stare. "Is it true, then, that you were sleeping with Gail Strickland?"

"Yes," admits Mitch. "But by the time I went out with Dee, it was over between Gail and me."

"It was over because of the note?"

"Yes. I suppose you could say that," says Mitch, not wanting to admit to the total truth.

"Exactly as I thought. I knew that Dee was interested in you. That she was determined to have you as her, I don't know…boyfriend. I know she was a very crafty lady, but I find it hard to believe she would stoop so low." Dr. Wynn's lips are quivering. She sits down in a chair.

"I don't have any proof," she goes on to say, "but it's possible Dee was responsible for that note. She visited me several months ago for no apparent reason. Spent an hour in her room. Came downstairs and asked for an envelope. One of my pink envelopes. That's pretty conclusive evidence, wouldn't you say?" She points at the pink envelope on the vanity top.

"Pretty conclusive," agrees Mitch.

"Then she asks to borrow the car. She's gone two hours, and, when she returns, I ask her where's she's been. 'To the post office to mail a letter,' she says. 'Then I met a friend. We had a drink at Republic.'"

"She could be telling the truth," suggests Mitch. Not that he wants to be the devil's advocate. He just doesn't want Dee's mother to think the worst of her. (He can't imagine what she thinks of him.)

"I don't know for sure," says Dr. Wynn. "It simply makes more sense that she was sneaking around Blair trying to plant that note in Ed Strickland's desk drawer.

"I mean, the police told me all about it. How Ed claimed there was a note planted in his desk but he didn't have it anymore. So they searched the house. Couldn't find it. Decided he was lying. I put two and two together. I figured since Gail probably saw the note, she might know where it is. I asked her, and she handed it over to me," says Dr. Wynn.

"But, you know, Mitch, I don't know what to do. I'd like to throw the note away. Forget it ever existed, because it might reflect poorly on my daughter. But that would be dishonest. Wouldn't it, Mitch?"

"I guess so." He looks at Dee's mother. She stares at him in her cold, doctorly fashion as though she wants to make him squirm.

"Yes, it would be dishonest," she says, still staring, though now it seems she can see through his skin. "And I suppose I can't be dishonest. I'll have to turn the note over to the police and hope for the best. Though I'd rather not. I'd rather see the worse thing possible happen to that man."

"Yes, ma'am."

They head downstairs in a slow, thoughtful way back to a couch in front of a much-diminished fire. Dr. Wynn pokes the wood. Pulls back the screen and tosses in a fresh piece. Mitch watches the blue flames lick the sides of the log as the fire flares up. It radiates a warmth through the room, makes him feel cozy and comfortable like in the Christmas song. Then he thinks about Dee, who will never experience this again.

The doctor excuses herself. She heads for the kitchen and comes back with a plate full of salted oatmeal cookies from the local co-op. Has she been consulting Kathy? Talk about crafty. She puts the plate on the coffee table. Mitch takes one.

"Thank you, Bev," he says, nibbling at the edges of the cookie. "My very favorite."

"You're welcome," she says sitting down beside him, almost too close, so that he has to move slightly to make room. She pours him another cup of tea and coffee for herself. She leans back. "I want to explain something very personal," she says in a halting tone as if, in fact, she doesn't. "I have a very scientific mind—as you may have guessed, since I am a doctor—but I'm also a bit on the emotional side when it comes to family. Take my husband, for example."

She explains that her husband was the only survivor of his rifle company at the Battle of the Bulge. "All his life he was plagued by guilt. It was like I married two men, the one with whom I raised our children and the one who left his buddies on the battlefield. He almost seemed happy to die." She starts crying. Mitch tries to comfort her, but she pushes him away.

"I tried to understand him in my scientific way, but I couldn't," she says, wiping her eyes. "I felt like it's my fault, some failure on my part that he didn't love me. That was the emotion getting in the way. But then, gradually, I changed my mind. Life is complicated. Gil loved me. He loved our children. He loved his job. We had a wonderful life together. He loved us so much that he was able to put aside his guilt in order to make us happy.

"Do you know anything about guilt?" she asks, looking at Mitch carefully as if she's trying to gauge his reaction. "Do you feel guilty about what happened to my daughter?"

Mitch looks down at his hands. "Yes."

"Well, you shouldn't feel that way any more than my husband felt guilty for surviving the Battle of the Bulge when his buddies in the rifle company didn't. Am I right?"

"Maybe you're right," says Mitch, trying to be honest. "But then there's the fact that Gail and I had an affair."

"Yes, true, but if Dee had not been so jealous as to write the note she stuffed in my pink envelope, then she would still be alive today and you would have no reason to feel guilty," she says, patting the space between them as if she were patting his hand. "And besides, it makes me wonder. Maybe I'm responsible for her death as well. The way I raised her. Too much emphasis on work. Too little on family. Then, at the end of her life, I changed my tune. I compared her to her happily married brothers and sisters. I made her feel like a lesser person. Besides, who knows? Maybe she expected too much out of men. Or maybe it was nature. Chance. God. Or all the above. It's enough to make my head spin."

Dr. Wynn takes a final sip of coffee and bangs the cup on the table with finality. "But the entire truth is," she says with furor, "there's only one person that I can blame for my daughter's murder. That's Ed Strickland. He is the real culprit. I hope he receives the punishment he deserves."

Mitch helps the doctor clear the table. He carries the plate stacked with finger sandwiches and the bowl of potato chips into the kitchen, one at a time since he only has the use of one hand. She carries the rest.

"I don't think we were very hungry," she says as she returns the chips to their bag. Clips the bag and places it in the refrigerator.

"I'll save these for the grandkids when they come over, though I don't think they are very healthy."

She stuffs the finger sandwiches and carrots and celery in a baggy and covers the dip with plastic wrap. Pours the tea and coffee in plastic containers. Returns all to the fridge.

"Waste not, want not," she says in an almost prissy voice. She puts the dishes in the sink. "I'll take care of those later. I have to do some work today."

She escorts him to the front door. They shake hands. Her eyes are red rimmed. He wants to hug her but doesn't dare. She holds her body so tightly, it's like she's surrounded by barbed wire.

He heads down the steps to his beat-up Saab. He climbs in and takes one last look at Dr. Wynn. She is standing erect at the half-open door with one hand on the handle, staring down at him with vacant eyes, as if he isn't really there. He cranks the engine, throws it in gear, and races up Sherman Avenue.

Epilogue

E d Strickland's lawyer, a friend of a Montgomery Blair
High School booster, begged the majority-male jury to
put themselves in Ed's place. What would you do if you
received an anonymous note that said your wife was having an
affair? What would you do if you suspected it was true? What
would you do if you suspected, after your wife ran off, she was
still sleeping with the man? Would you sit there and take it?
Or would you try to recover what was stolen from you? And
when Ed Strickland decided to confront the thief, how was he
to know that the person coming down the stairs was a woman
and not Mitch Lovett? He couldn't see clearly. He fired the gun
wildly. Wounded both Mitch Lovett and Dee Wynn. And this
was the crux of the matter: Ed Strickland wounded Dee Wynn.
Wounded her. He didn't kill her. He didn't even want to fire
a gun in anger at Dee Wynn. But he did. He wounded her.
She lost her balance and toppled down the stairs at the mercy
of gravity. She hit her head against the newel post, and that's
what killed her. Not the shotgun blast, but her head coming
into contact with the post. Sure, it was tragic Ed Strickland
went to such lengths to right a wrong. That he took the law
into his own hands. That Dee Wynn got caught in the middle.
Tragic. But not tragic enough to condemn this man to a life in
prison, a man who was driven crazy by his wife's infidelity. If
you are to condemn Ed Strickland, the defense claimed, then
you must condemn all those involved in this case: the wife,
the lover, and the writer of the note. You must even condemn
gravity itself.

The prosecution's argument was that, though Ed Strickland
intended to murder Mitch Lovett and he ended up murdering
Dee Wynn, it was still murder in the first degree. The Maryland

code describes murder in the first degree as a "deliberate, premeditated, and willful killing." The prosecution went on to say, "The defendant's lawyer can obfuscate this murder with all his fancy language, but he cannot obscure his client's intent to murder another human being."

No matter what the prosecution's argument, the case was open and shut to the jury. Ed Strickland did not with "deliberate, premeditated, and willful aforethought" kill Dee Wynn. It was an accident. Therefore, Ed was guilty of murder in the second degree.

A year and half after they shipped Ed Strickland to Jessup for thirty years, the maximum sentence in Maryland, Gail called Mitch and asked him if he was still available.

"Yes, I'm available," he said.

They decided to meet a week later at her condo in McLean Gardens and then go out to dinner. Mitch found a Civil War mess kit at an antique store in Fredericksburg, Virginia, and handed it to Gail when she opened her door.

"This must've cost you a fortune," she said nervously.

"Worth every cent."

"You're a sweetheart," she laughed and dragged him off to dinner. Afterward, back home, they resumed where they left off.

Six months later they were married at the county courthouse on Groundhog Day. They purchased a bungalow in Buckeystown, Maryland, down the block from the antique mall that they had visited a lifetime ago, it seemed, when they were returning from their tryst at the Antietam Inn full of dread. It was amazing, they thought—a house for sale, and for a song, Mitch believed, leaving them enough money left over from the sale of the property on Oak Lane to rent a stall at the antique mall. Gail was elated. She filled her stall with Craftsman, art deco, and Civil War era antiques. Sales were brisk. She rented another stall. She didn't make a fortune, but she was comfortable. She was in her element.

Mitch found a job in Frederick, ten miles distant and a straight shot down 270 to Washington. The only thing that upset the couple was that Davy hated his new life. He missed his old playmates. But in the houses on either side of him were young families with children and nearby acres and acres of woods to play in. They hoped, in time, he'd grow to love it as much as they did.

Gail was pregnant. She was ecstatic. "This is the happiest moment of my life," she told Mitch. "Well, as happy as I was with Davy, but in another way. For the first time in my life, I'm having a baby with a man I truly love and who truly loves me for who I am."

Mitch worried because he knew what had happened to Gail in Colorado. Though Davy's had been a normal birth, she was older now. He wasn't going to take chances. So he studied the route to the hospital. Some mornings he drove to work at breakneck speed to see how long it would take to get to Frederick Memorial, where the baby was to be born. He stopped at the five lights along the way. Counted how long it took them to change, a total of eight and half minutes. If he traveled an average of fifty miles an hour, sixty or seventy on the straightaways, it would take him maybe twenty-five minutes to reach the hospital. He told Gail, and she said he was crazy, but, as it turned out, he was right.

Seven months into her pregnancy, Gail woke up at five a.m. She felt something wet and sticky between her legs.

"I'm bleeding," she screamed.

Mitch jumped out of bed. Turned on the light. Looked down. "Oh, my God." He fought back an urge to panic, not too successfully, because it was Gail who called the doctor. He told them to come immediately.

Mitch woke up Davy. He grabbed a bunch of towels from the bathroom. They jumped in their clothes. Didn't bother to brush their teeth or comb their hair. Rushed downstairs to the Saab and raced up Buckeystown Pike. It took him eighteen minutes. He ran every light except for one. At one intersection, there were two cars waiting while a third one turned left. He squeezed around to the right between a telephone pole and fireplug. He ran over a bush. Scraped the passenger-side door against a fence before he sped across the road, the cars honking behind him.

"That was cool," said Davy, shaking his head approvingly at Mitch's driving acumen.

The doctor was waiting at the hospital. They wheeled Gail into the operating area. Mitch sat down, Davy next to him. They looked at each other. Scared.

An hour later, the doctor came out. "Both your wife and the baby are fine, though we took the baby to the neonatal unit as a precaution. She's premature, you know, but I don't believe you need to worry. She scored normal on the Apgar test."

A month later they took the baby home. Gail was worried that, after all this time away from her, she'd have problems bonding with the child. But the moment she laid the baby down in the cradle next to their bed and she saw the heart-shaped lips, the hazel eyes, and the ridge of freckles across her tiny nose, she burst into tears.

"She looks exactly like I imagined. Like the baby I lost."

They named her Sarah. They were happy. They couldn't believe how happy they were. They gave a party. Invited all the Stork Club members. They saw Bob and Kathy's new baby. Sonya was pregnant with her second child. Robin was thinking about adopting a child of one of her patients since Barry had quit his job at the Saab dealership and found a more lucrative one at BMW. Barry told Mitch that Bull married his girlfriend, Paula Wells, and moved to Garrett County where he worked in the family meat-packing business.

"We'll stay in Takoma Park forever," said Barry, shaking his head, sadly. "It's home, though we'll miss you guys who moved away. It won't seem the same."

Mitch was flipping hamburgers at the grill in the backyard while Barry was waiting eagerly with a plate, the empty bun yawning open. "I like them medium rare," he said pointing at one with the juices pouring out. Mitch flipped it onto his bun. Barry wandered over to the condiment table, piled on lettuce, tomato, onion, mustard, ketchup, relish, and pickle, and wandered back.

"You have a wonderful place here," he said, as he tried to open his mouth wide enough to encompass the hamburger. "That's one good thing. We'll come to visit. And whenever you're in town, you visit us."

"Yeah, sure. I'll do that," said Mitch, piling a plate full of hamburgers and taking it to the table before he put more on the grill. He glanced across the field to the horizon where the sun was setting behind the trees, turning the underside of the clouds pink. On the other side of a fence where the farmland started, a cow was mooing for all it was worth. Sometimes in the morning, he would hear the same cow, or maybe it was another one—dozens of cows dotted the fields, mooing plaintively. It was a dairy cow—he could tell by the udders. What she needed was milking, but she was lost to the rest of the herd and couldn't find the trail back to the barn. Mitch thought about this. He thought about some mornings the cow wouldn't be there and he'd hear far off a rooster crowing or a dog barking or the hum of the traffic on I-270 two miles off, but not much else, a near-perfect silence that made him edgy.

When the party was over and they waved good-bye to the last Stork Club member, he and Gail cleared the dishes and carried them inside. "Can you believe we'll be living here for the rest of our lives?" said Gail. The way she smiled, radiantly, she didn't seem bothered at all by this possibility.

A few days later Mitch drives down to pick up the kids at Bob's house in Georgetown where they moved after they sold the bungalow. He detours to New Hampshire Avenue. He doesn't turn in at Oak Lane because the house is gone, as is the oak tree beside it—the whole forest, as a matter of fact, all gone, despite the efforts of tree hugging protesters, the town arborist, and the Takoma Park Tree Commission.

When he drives back that night with Addie and Julian, he's exhausted. They eat dinner. Davy talks about the fort they are going to build the next morning. "There's a big tree out back with two huge branches that fork out. We'll build a platform on top of the fork. Then we'll build the sides and the roof on the ground. Lift them up by a block and tackle attached to another branch above the platform. Attach it all to the platform, and we're finished. I know it'll work because Mitch promised to help."

Addie and Julian laugh.

"What's so funny?" asks Davy.

"You calling our dad Mitch," says Addie.

Mitch and Gail herd the kids upstairs. The kids all sleep in one room in the front of the house overlooking an expansive lawn and a pine tree that is so tall it bends at the top. Mitch reads two chapters of *The Wind in the Willows* before they fall asleep.

He trudges into the bedroom in the back of the house. Gail is lying in bed reading a book. He kisses her good night and slips under the covers beside her. He falls asleep instantly. During the night, he dreams of Dee Wynn lying at the bottom of the stairs, her body twisted like a Barbie doll. He wakes with a start.

Gail is sitting in a rocking chair beside the window feeding Sarah. Behind her the moon shines above the treetops, bathing mother and child in a ghostly light.

"You had one of your dreams again, didn't you?" asks Gail, in a subdued voice, looking up from her feeding.

"Yes, I did."

"I wish you didn't have those kinds of dreams," she says, an edge to her voice. He doesn't want her to cry.

"I wish I didn't either. But I can't help it."

"I know. I'm sorry."

"No need to be," says Mitch. He sits up in bed, smiles at her. "You're my lady."

THE END